SCULPTING MEN

SCULPTING MEN

A COMPLETE GUIDE FOR MEN'S MINISTRY & LEADERSHIP

Vince Miller

EQUIP PRESS

Colorado Springs

SCULPTING MEN

Copyright © 2024 Vince Miller

All rights reserved. No part of this publication may be reproduced, distributed, or transmitted in any form or by any means, without prior written permission.

Published by Equip Press, Colorado Springs, CO

Scripture quotations marked (ESV) are taken from The ESV® Bible (The Holy Bible, English Standard Version®) copyright © 2001 by Crossway, a publishing ministry of Good News Publishers. ESV® Text Edition: 2011. The ESV® text has been reproduced in cooperation with and by permission of Good News Publishers. Unauthorized reproduction of this publication is prohibited. Used by permission. All rights reserved.

Scripture quotations marked (KJV) are taken from the King James Bible. Accessed on Bible Gateway at www.BibleGateway.com.

Scripture quotations marked (NASB) are taken from the New American Standard Bible® (NASB), copyright © 1960, 1962, 1963, 1968, 1971, 1972, 1973, 1975, 1977, 1995 by The Lockman Foundation, www.Lockman.org. Used by permission.

Scripture quotations marked (NIV) are taken from the Holy Bible, New International Version. Copyright © 1973, 1978, 1984, 2011 by Biblica, Inc.® Used by permission. All rights reserved worldwide.

Scripture quotations marked (NKJV) are taken from the New King James Version®. Copyright © 1982 by Thomas Nelson, Inc. Used by permission. All rights reserved.

Scripture quotations marked (NLT) are taken from the Holy Bible, New Living Translation, copyright © 1996, 2004, 2015 by Tyndale House Foundation. Used by permission of Tyndale House Publishers, Inc., Carol Stream, Illinois 60188. All rights reserved.

Scripture quotations marked (NRSV) are taken from the New Revised Standard Version Bible, copyright © 1989 the Division of Christian Education of the National Council of the Churches of Christ in the United States of America. Used by permission. All rights reserved.

First Edition: 2024
Sculpting Men / Vince Miller
Paperback ISBN: 978-1-958585-76-4
eBook ISBN: 978-1-958585-77-1

EQUIP PRESS
Colorado Springs

DEDICATION

To every man who has invested in me. Thank you.
I love every one of you.
Your investment will pay eternal dividends you may never see,
but God knows.

CONTENTS

Introduction 11

Section 1: Foundations of Men's Ministry and Leadership

7 Reasons Men Are The Most Strategic Method to Impacting Everything 15
A Vision Will Strengthen Your Ministry To Men 19
5 Crucial Reasons To Disciple And Develop Men 25
Commitment is Critical: If You Are Going To Start, You Better
    Be Committed 29
Building a Partnership with Your Pastor in Men's Ministry 35
3 New Strategies for Building a Thriving Men's Ministry 39
5 Proposals That Cultivate Biblical Manhood In Your Church 43
Why Men Have Trouble Opening Up (and What To Do) 47
The Case For Mentoring Men In Your Church 53
Guiding Men From Shame To Grace To Freedom 55
7 Character Challenges Men Encounter 59
Calling Men Into an Adventurous Faith 63

Section 2: Mentorship & Discipleship

3 Marks: That Will Accelerate Men & Your Ministry To Men 69
Mentorship: The Cornerstone of Building Men in Faith 73
Enlisting Others: The Collective Effort of Men's Ministry 77
Train & Prepare A Wingman 81
4 Traits for Becoming An Effective Mentor & Men's Leader 85
Mentors Ask The Best Questions 89
5 Keys To Mentoring Relationships 93
6 Steps To Finding A Mentor & 3 Types of Mentors 99
The Gradual Release Model: A Journey For Mentoring & Leading 105
The Framework of Spiritual Mentoring: Structuring the Experience 109

The K.M.S. Mindset For Mentoring & Building Men 113
God's Word Is Essential For A Man's Growth: It's the Guide 117
Five Disciplines To Build Into Every Man.. 121
Building & Sustaining A Quiet Time With God 127
Building a Bible-Reading Habit.. 131
Get Godly Advice as a Man and Leader.. 133
The Importance of Accountability For Men... 137
6 Prescriptions for the Godly Man 141
Helping Men Battle Hurts, Habits, & Hang-ups.. 145
For God's Sake, Let Your Men Pray... 149
Shoulder to Shoulder: The Missing Link for Men 151

Section 3: Practical Tools for Ministry To Men

Recruiting Men: The 3 M's.. 157
Ministry: Starting a Men's Ministry In A Small Church 161
Ministry: Starting A Men's Ministry In A Mid-Sized Church 165
Ministry: Pay Attention to A Man's Pain.. 169
Ministry: Qualifications For Men's Leaders... 175
Ministry: Fundamentals For The Spiritual Leader.. 181
Ministry: 3 Challenges To Expect In Leading Men... 185
Ministry: Dealing With Conflict.. 189
Ministry: 4 Pointers For Planning A Men's Retreat 193
Groups: 4 Fail-Proof Ways to Keep Men Engaged.. 197
Groups: Top Reasons Men Don't Join Men's Groups 201
Groups: The Inductive O.I.A. Method for Bible Study 207
Groups: The S.O.A.P. Method for Bible Study 209
Groups: A Sample of a 60-Minute S.O.A.P. Study.. 213
Groups: A Step-By-Step Guide To A First Group Meeting 215
Groups: 10 Creative Formats For a Men's Small Group 219
Groups: 6 Expectations For Every Man In A Small Group............................. 223
Groups: Best to Worst Small Group Locations 227
Groups: H.O.T. Men Make Stronger Connections 233

In Closing: What's Your Lane? 237

ABOUT VINCE MILLER

Vince Miller was born in Vallejo, California. At twenty, he made a profession of faith while in college and felt a strong, sudden call to work in full-time ministry. After college and graduate school, he invested two decades working with notable ministries like Young Life, InterVarsity Christian Fellowship and in senior leadership within the local church. He currently resides in St. Paul, Minnesota, with his wife, Christina. They have three adult children.

Then in March 2014, he founded Resolute out of his passion for discipleship and leadership development of men. This passion was born out of his personal need for growth. Vince turned everywhere to find a man who would mentor, disciple, and develop him throughout his spiritual life. He often received two answers from well-meaning Christian leaders: *either they did not know what to do in a mentoring relationship, or they did not have the time to do it.* Vince learned that he was not alone. Many Christian men were seeking this type of mentorship relationship. Therefore, he felt compelled to build an organization that would focus on two things: ensuring that men who want to be discipled have the opportunity and that they have real tools to disciple other men.

Vince is an authentic and transparent leader who loves to communicate with men and has a deep passion for God's Word. He has authored several dozen books, and he is the primary content creator of all Resolute content and discipleship materials.

INTRODUCTION

In the journey of faith, leadership is not just a role, but a divine calling—a sculpting process that molds men into the image God desires. As a seasoned guide for this transformative journey, I bring to you *Sculpting Men: A Complete Guide for Men's Ministry and Leadership*, a culmination of over three decades of dedicated ministry and leadership experience. But this book is not just a compilation of theories; it is a reservoir of practical wisdom born from the trenches of real-life ministry to men.

In the pages that follow we will embark on a comprehensive exploration of what it takes to build and lead a thriving men's ministry. This book offers a roadmap for those who are called to lead men toward spiritual maturity and godly manhood. From the foundational principles of men's ministry to the intricate dynamics of mentorship and discipleship, each chapter is a carefully laid stone in the path of building effective and transformative ministry to men.

Sculpting Men is composed of three sections, each addressing a core aspect of men's ministry and leadership. In the first section, "Foundations of Men's Ministry and Leadership," we dig into the strategic importance of men in the church, the power of vision in strengthening men's ministry, and the indispensable role of commitment and partnership with pastoral leadership. This section sets the stage, laying out the "why" and "how" of engaging men in a meaningful and impactful way.

The second section, "Mentorship & Discipleship," is the heart of the journey, where we uncover the art and science of shaping men's lives through mentorship. Here we explore the qualities of effective mentors, the dynamics of mentoring relationships, and the transformative power of God's Word in men's growth. This section is a treasure trove of insights for anyone looking to mentor men or be mentored, offering practical strategies and real-life examples.

In the final section, "Practical Tools for Ministry To Men," we catalyze action. This section is packed with hands-on tools and approaches for various aspects of men's ministry, from recruiting and leading men to facilitating engaging group studies and managing conflicts. It's a comprehensive guide for both budding and experienced leaders seeking to navigate the challenges and triumphs of men's ministry.

Each chapter of *Sculpting Men* is a testament to the challenges, victories, and lessons learned in my decades of ministry to men. This book is not just for reading; it is for action. It is an invitation to join a movement of men committed to being sculpted into the likeness of Christ, men who will rise to the call of leadership, mentorship, and discipleship in their communities and beyond.

As you turn these pages, my prayer is that you will be inspired, equipped, and transformed. Whether you are starting a new men's ministry, seeking to revitalize an existing one, or looking to grow personally as a leader and disciple-maker, *Sculpting Men* is your guide. Together, let's embark on this journey of sculpting men for God's glory and the advancement of His kingdom.

SECTION 1

FOUNDATIONS OF MEN'S MINISTRY AND LEADERSHIP

7 REASONS MEN ARE THE MOST STRATEGIC METHOD TO IMPACTING EVERYTHING

By investing in men's spiritual and personal growth, we uncover a transformative power that radiates across seven key areas of life. This commitment to building up men doesn't merely lead to individual enhancement; it unleashes a cascade of positive effects that touch every corner of society. From strengthening the family unit to reshaping community dynamics and invigorating church involvement, the implications are profound and far-reaching.

Let's explore the seven different effects of building up men, each representing a critical pillar in the overarching mission of creating a more resilient and faithful society.

First | Fortifying Families Through Men's Growth: Solid, faith-anchored men are the bedrock of stable, loving families. By comprehending and embracing their roles within the family and community, men become influential catalysts for positive change, fostering a more healthy and upright society.

Second | Countering Cultural Disorientation: In an era riddled with conflicting narratives about masculinity, men often find themselves adrift. The church stands as a beacon, offering a clear, Christ-centered blueprint of manhood. This clarity imbues men with a sense of direction and a deeper purpose.

Third | Revitalizing Men's Role in Church Life: The dwindling participation of men, particularly young adult men, in church activities is a pressing concern. Actively engaging men in the fabric of church life and entrusting them with substantive roles can help reverse this worrying trend.

Fourth | Instilling Purpose and Direction: Men, in the absence of an inspiring and meaningful life vision, may turn to detrimental pursuits. The church is poised to provide an elevating, hope-filled perspective, steering men toward acts of service, leadership, and spiritual maturity.

Fifth | Empowering Men to Expand God's Mission: Prioritizing men's spiritual development is a strategic move for the growth of the church. When men are grounded in their faith they emerge as leaders, fostering a vibrant, expanding community of believers.

Sixth | Cultivating Pastors and Leaders: Understanding the pivotal role of engaging men, church leaders can greatly benefit from a straightforward, practical strategy aimed at cultivating strong, faithful men. This effort can have a transformative impact on their congregations and beyond.

Seventh | Transforming Broader Communities: Men who are fortified in their faith and understanding can create a ripple effect of positive change. They evolve into exemplary fathers, husbands, and civic leaders, inspiring and influencing their surroundings, which leads to wider societal transformation.

In conclusion, the comprehensive development of strong men for ministry is not just a singular goal but a multi-layered strategy. It reinforces family bonds, confronts cultural misconceptions, reinvigorates men's involvement in church, and raises a new generation of leaders. This holistic investment extends beyond personal growth, contributing to the enrichment of the entire church, community, and society at large.

A VISION WILL STRENGTHEN YOUR MINISTRY TO MEN

Crafting a vision statement is a crucial step in developing your ministry to men. This doesn't matter if you are leading one man, a group of men, or plan on reaching the planet with your ministry. (And I do hope you choose to reach the planet!)

A statement of vision is more than just words; it's the heartbeat of your unique ministry. The following are some things you should think about as you develop your vision.

One | Start With Your Core Values & Beliefs: Think deeply about what drives you. What foundational Christian values and beliefs are you building this ministry upon? These are non-negotiable and should be deeply rooted in your understanding of scripture and theology.

Two | Picture the Future: Imagine the ultimate impact of your ministry. What does success look like for you and the men you're aiming to reach? It could be about spiritual growth, community impact, or personal transformations. Be specific about what it looks like and what a man might look like at the end.

Three | Set The Bar Higher Than Your Reach: Your vision should be a beacon of inspiration, pushing you and the men in your ministry to stretch beyond the comfort zone, yet remain achievable. It should stir excitement and a sense of higher calling. But if it's not God-sized you will try to do it all on your own.

Four | Be Clear & Concise: Your vision statement should be a clear, concise beacon that guides you. It needs to be memorable and straightforward - a couple of sentences that capture the essence of your ambition.

Five | Imagine the Man at the End: Remember, it's about what you aim to achieve, not how you'll get there. The "how" comes later when you're planning strategies and actions.

Six | Involve Other Men: Since ministry is all about community, get input from others who share your passion. This way, your vision is not just yours but shared, resonating with everyone involved.

Seven | Write It Out: Put pen to paper and start drafting. Don't stress about perfection on your first go. Write your vision, then refine it to something that truly speaks to the heart of your mission.

Eight | Tell It and Live It: Once you've nailed it down, share this vision with everyone involved. It's vital that they grasp and embrace this vision, as it will guide all your future actions and decisions.

Remember, your vision statement might pivot or adjust. As your ministry grows and evolves, so too might your vision. It's your north star, keeping your mission aligned and focused.

Do a little work right now and answer these questions:

1. **Start With Your Core Values & Beliefs:** What core Christian values and beliefs anchor your ministry? How do these values shape the mission and activities of your ministry?

2. **Picture the Future:** Imagine the long-term impact of your men's ministry. What specific transformations do you hope to see in the lives of the men involved? How does this vision of change guide your planning and approach?

3. **Set the Bar Higher Than Your Reach:** What ambitious, "God-sized" goal do you have for your men's ministry that pushes you and others beyond your comfort zones? How does this goal reflect your faith in God's power and purpose for the ministry?

4. **Be Clear & Concise:** In a few concise sentences, how would you articulate the vision of your men's ministry? How does this clear statement serve as a guiding beacon for you and the men involved?

5. **Imagine the Man at the End:** Envision a man who has been transformed through your ministry. What qualities, characteristics, and spiritual maturity does he possess? How does this vision shape your ministry's focus and activities?

6. **Involve Other Men:** Who are the men in your community whose input and collaboration could enrich the vision of your ministry? How can you involve them to ensure the vision resonates with and is owned by the wider group?

7. **Write It Out:** Take time to draft the vision statement for your men's ministry. What key elements emerge in this initial version? How do these elements align with the overarching mission of the ministry?

8. **Tell It and Live It:** How do you plan to communicate and embody the vision of your men's ministry? What actions will you take to ensure this vision is actively lived out in the ministry's activities and culture?

Now, write your unforgettable vision statement below. Make it simple and repeatable. If it's not, you won't remember it, and neither will others.

5 CRUCIAL REASONS TO DISCIPLE AND DEVELOP MEN

In a world where men often find themselves adrift in the sea of life, it becomes abundantly clear that they need more than just casual guidance. They require intentional direction, a solid foundation in truth, the camaraderie of brotherhood, the wisdom that only life experience can offer, and a challenge that propels them toward their fullest potential. Drawing inspiration from the timeless wisdom of the Scriptures and the deliberate example set by Jesus Christ, in this exploration, we will dig into the five crucial reasons why building men is not just a noble endeavor but an essential one, touching the lives of countless men and guiding them toward becoming the best version of themselves.

Reason One: Men Need Intentional Direction

> *When he went ashore he saw a great crowd, and he had compassion on them, because they were like sheep without a shepherd. And he began to teach them many things. — Mark 6:34*

In Mark 6:34, we witness a poignant moment when Jesus, upon seeing a great crowd, had compassion on them because they were like sheep without a shepherd. He began to teach them many things. This reveals a fundamental truth: men need intentional direction.

While it's possible for a man to receive mentorship and discipline without a formal plan, we must remember that Jesus' approach to discipling the twelve was far from accidental. It was deliberate, methodical, and purposeful. We can't simply rely on casual interactions with other men; we need a structured plan to guide us on our journey of growth.

Reason Two: Men Need The Truth

All Scripture is breathed out by God and profitable for teaching, for reproof, for correction, and for training in righteousness, that the man of God may be complete, equipped for every good work.
— 2 Timothy 3:16-17

Men hunger for a deep understanding of the Bible and the God it reveals. While your insights are valuable, they should always echo the truth found in God's Word. Our relationship with God takes precedence over any other. Your role as a guide is crucial, but it's vital to steer men toward the ultimate source of truth: the scriptures.

Reason Three: Men Need Accountability In Brotherhood

And let us consider how to stir up one another to love and good works, not neglecting to meet together, as is the habit of some, but encouraging one another, and all the more as you see the Day drawing near.
— Hebrews 10:24-25

Hebrews 10:24-25 emphasizes the importance of meeting together and encouraging one another. It's common for men to prefer autonomy and anonymity, but these tendencies can hinder greatness. Accountability within a brotherhood can lead to remarkable transformations in a man's life. We simply cannot navigate the spiritual journey alone. By standing alongside other men, sharing struggles and victories, we can overcome our tendencies to withdraw and find the support needed to grow in our faith.

Reason Four: Men Need Life Wisdom

Blessed is the one who finds wisdom, and the one who gets understanding, for the gain from her is better than gain from silver and her profit better than gold. She is more precious than jewels, and nothing you desire can compare with her. — Proverbs 3:13-15

Proverbs 3:13-15 extols the value of wisdom, describing it as more precious than silver, gold, or jewels. Every man desires the wisdom that comes from seasoned individuals. It's a hunger that can be seen in the original twelve disciples who sought wisdom from Jesus.

The blessing of an older man pouring life wisdom into a younger one is something every man longs for. This wisdom isn't just theoretical; it's practical guidance for navigating the complexities of life and faith.

Reason Five: Men Need A Challenge

If anyone comes to me and does not hate his own father and mother and wife and children and brothers and sisters, yes, and even his own life, he cannot be my disciple. — Luke 14:26

In Luke 14:26, Jesus sets a high bar for discipleship, challenging us to prioritize our commitment to Him above all else, even our closest relationships. This reveals that men need a challenge.

By raising the bar and presenting a vision that aligns with Christ's calling, men are inspired to step up and become better versions of themselves. The challenge should not be about following your vision, but rather Christ's vision for their lives, a challenge that ignites their inner drive to excel.

In conclusion, these five reasons underscore the importance of your work in building men. It's about intentional direction, grounding in truth, fostering brotherhood and accountability, sharing life wisdom, and presenting challenging visions. Through your guidance, men can grow and become the best versions of themselves, aligned with Christ's calling.

COMMITMENT IS CRITICAL: IF YOU ARE GOING TO START, YOU BETTER BE COMMITTED

In my years of experience with men's ministry I've witnessed a concerning trend: many men start their journey with enthusiasm and determination, yet, sadly, a significant number falter along the way. This pattern of initial commitment followed by a gradual decline (or abrupt halt) is not just disheartening, it underscores a deeper issue within the realm of spiritual leadership and personal growth. The excitement of new beginnings often masks the challenges that lie ahead—challenges that test faith, resolve, and the very core of a man's character. It's a phenomenon that reveals the need for more than just good intentions; it calls for a sustained, resilient commitment, a kind that endures through trials and evolves over time. As a leader in this field, I've dedicated myself to understanding and addressing the root causes of why so many begin this vital journey with vigor only to lose their way and how we, as a community of faith, can better support and guide these men towards lasting fulfillment in their spiritual walk.

Based on my observations in men's ministry, several common reasons why men may discontinue their involvement include:

One | Lack of Time or Over-Commitment: Many men find it challenging to balance the demands of work, family, and ministry. This struggle often leads to feeling overwhelmed, resulting in their withdrawal from ministry activities.

Two | Unmet Expectations: Some men enter ministry with specific expectations about personal growth, spiritual experiences, or community dynamics. When these expectations are not met, they can become discouraged and choose to leave.

Three | Difficulty in Forming Deep Connections: Men often seek meaningful relationships and mentorship in ministry settings. If they struggle to forge these connections, they may feel isolated or undervalued and eventually lose interest.

Four | Challenges in Personal Life: Personal crises, such as family issues, health problems, or financial stress, can divert focus and energy away from ministry involvement.

Five | Lack of Visible Progress or Impact: Men may become disheartened if they don't perceive tangible progress in their spiritual journey or see a direct impact of their efforts in the ministry.

Six | Moral or Ethical Challenges: Encounters with personal moral failings or disillusionment with the behavior of others in the ministry can lead to a crisis of faith or integrity, prompting some to step back.

Seven | Burnout: Continuous engagement without adequate rest or support can lead to burnout, causing men to feel exhausted and necessitating a step back from ministry activities.

Eight | Cultural or Generational Differences: Differences in viewpoints or approaches between various age groups or cultural backgrounds can create misunderstandings or conflicts, leading some men to feel out of place.

Nine | Insufficient Support or Guidance: A lack of mentorship, guidance, or support from ministry leaders can leave men feeling directionless and unsupported in their spiritual journey.

Understanding and addressing these challenges is crucial in creating a more supportive and enduring men's ministry environment. But each of these challenges in men's ministry demands a heads-on strategy and mindset rooted in resilience and unwavering commitment.

Here are five principles that will build your endurance and commitment as you begin:

One | An Undeniable Focus on God: First and foremost, center every aspect of your ministry and life around God. This isn't just about participating in ministry activities; it's about ensuring that every action, every decision, and every interaction is a reflection of our devotion to Him. When God is at the core of all we do we set our course with greater clarity and purpose. If you are focused on your will, you are sure to fail.

Two | Set Realistic Expectations: Step into ministry with your eyes wide open. Realize that true growth and impact are marathons, not sprints. Keep your fire burning, even when immediate results aren't in sight. Adaptability is key – be ready to take on various roles and responsibilities. This keeps your involvement dynamic and meaningful, and you won't feel like a failure if you fail once in a while.

Three | Forge Strong, Authentic Connections: The cornerstone of a thriving men's ministry is the forging of deep, real relationships. I urge you to engage in open, honest dialogue, to be vulnerable, and to support one another. This is how we build a brotherhood, a fellowship where every man has a pillar to lean on through thick and thin. It's these bonds that fortify our commitment to the cause. Fragile connections will not fortify your ministry or your resolve.

Four | Take Care of Yourself: Your spiritual well-being is as critical as your physical and mental health. I cannot stress enough the importance of self-care. Dedicate time for personal reflection, prayer, and rest. This isn't just about avoiding burnout; it's about maintaining a harmonious balance between our ministry duties and our personal lives.

Five | Cultivate a Culture of Mentorship and Mutual Support: Integrating a strong mentorship framework can transform our ministry. Seasoned mentors offer not just guidance and wisdom but also an empathetic ear. They are navigators helping newer members steer through the turbulent waters. Let's also foster an environment where every man feels comfortable sharing his battles and seeking assistance. It's this kind of supportive atmosphere that bolsters our ministry's resilience and efficacy. Remember if it's all about you, you are sure to fail.

In conclusion, the hurdles we face in men's ministry are undeniably real and diverse. However, they are far from unbeatable. Approaching these challenges with a steadfast, committed mindset and supporting each other every step of the way is how we build a ministry that's not only enduring but also profoundly influences our personal and spiritual journeys. Stand firm, men, for this is the path to our collective strength and growth.

BUILDING A PARTNERSHIP WITH YOUR PASTOR IN MEN'S MINISTRY

Partnership with your pastor is always important. Too many men make the mistake of thinking you don't need a pastor to partner with you. But you do. That is, unless you are building your ministry outside of the church. Which is fine, too. But even then you are eventually going to have to partner with a pastor. (Unless that pastor is a heretic, then don't bother.)

But even so, we should all understand and support pastors. Our spiritual shepherds carry a heavy load, one that can sometimes be invisible to us. By knowing the challenges pastors face, especially concerning men's ministry, we can foster a better and deeper partnership with them, paving the way for a more effective and transformative ministry among men.

Here are a couple of things to keep in mind:

One | Your Pastor Is Probably Privately Burdened & Overwhelmed: Imagine being at the helm of a ship, navigating through uncharted waters, and responsible for the well-being of everyone on board. This analogy is the role of a pastor. They are tasked with delivering insightful sermons, providing pastoral care, and overseeing various church activities. This relentless tide of responsibilities often leaves pastors stretched thin, wrestling with the guilt of not being able to dedicate more time and energy to specific ministries, including men's ministry. This overwhelming sense of duty can sometimes lead to burnout, impacting their ability to serve effectively.

Two | Ministry Is A Daunting Task, Even More So Men's Ministry: Within the spectrum of church ministries, men's ministry presents its unique set of challenges. It's not merely a matter of scarce time or limited resources; it involves addressing the distinctive spiritual needs of men, which can be complex and multifaceted. This complexity can be daunting for pastors, making them hesitant to explore and launch it.

Recognizing and addressing these challenges is not just an act of empathy towards our pastors but a strategic step in building a thriving men's ministry. We need to remember that our pastors are not just leaders but human beings who need our support and understanding. By acknowledging and alleviating some of their burdens, we can collaboratively work towards nurturing a dynamic and spiritually enriching men's ministry.

Here is how I would forge a relationship and partnership with them:

4 Principles for Forging a Partnership With Your Pastor

One | Initiate a Conversation: Start by inviting your pastor out for lunch. This informal setting can provide a comfortable atmosphere for open discussion.

Two | Build Vision Together: During your meeting, seek to understand his vision for the men in the church. This is a crucial step. Knowing where he stands and what he aims to achieve can help you align your efforts with his.

Three | Offer Your Leadership & Support in Small Ways: Begin by identifying small, manageable ways to support his vision. These initial steps are vital in building trust and demonstrating your commitment to the church's goals.

Four | Let Him Leverage Your Unique Skills: Share with your pastor how your specific talents and skills could benefit the men's ministry. This could range from leading small groups, organizing events, or even offering mentorship.

Be Patient

Building a strong partnership with your pastor is often a gradual process. While it's natural to want to jump in and make things happen quickly, remember that meaningful change takes time. Serving the community and supporting the vision of the church through your pastor is a significant aspect of men's ministry. This support can sometimes be the most impactful work you do.

By understanding your pastor's challenges and aligning your efforts with his vision, you can create a robust and effective partnership. This collaboration not only strengthens the men's ministry but also contributes to the overall health and growth of the church. Remember, partnering with your pastor is not just about achieving goals; it's about walking together in faith and building a community that reflects the love and teachings of Jesus Christ.

3 NEW STRATEGIES FOR BUILDING A THRIVING MEN'S MINISTRY

I love it when men are eager to establish a ministry for men in their church. This zeal and dedication are worth celebrating, not sidelining. It's immediately noticeable in the church how every other ministry thrives (such as those for children, teens, women, and even the quilting club) while the involvement of men, across all age groups, remains notably low. Don't just take my word for it, the statistics speak for themselves.

Church surveys have long noted the gender gap in American congregations. One account placed the disparity of church-attending adults at 61% female versus 31%–and that figure may be low.

This may be unsettling for some, but it's not a new trend. It has persisted for centuries. However, I share your belief that we can change this. From my 28 years in ministry, I have gleaned insights and strategies that have been instrumental in developing and sustaining a men's ministry.

First | The Men You Want May Not Be In The Church
Indeed, the very reason you're reading this is that men are absent.

We need to shift our mindset when it comes to reaching out to men. Men's ministry doesn't conform to the typical approaches used in other church initiatives. I've observed ministry leaders mistakenly assume that, like women's ministry, men will respond to invitations – but that's not usually the case. Men require a different approach, a unique strategy. Before you start planning, consider this statistic about your target audience, as it offers valuable insights about men.

Fact About A Man's Engagement With The Church:

> "Over 90 percent of American men believe in God, and five out of six identify as Christians. But only one in six attends church on a given Sunday. The average man acknowledges Jesus Christ but doesn't see the value in church attendance." (Barna, "Women are the Backbone of Christian Congregations in America.")

This fact should be pondered deeply, as it highlights two significant challenges. First, many Christian men are content with their current spiritual state, leading to a pervasive sin among men - apathy. Second, efforts to engage men during weekend services will likely miss five out of six men. Accepting this reality is crucial; it's where we need to start thinking more strategically.

When building a men's ministry, these two facts are your foundation. You can't change them, but you can adapt your approach in light of them. If men aren't coming to you, it's time to find innovative ways to reach them.

Here's an Idea — Leading With Power. Founded in Wisconsin by Keith Tompkins, Leading With Power is a successful example of men's ministry. It has attracted hundreds of men across multiple locations with a simple, effective model. Each month, men from various backgrounds are invited to a meal and a talk. These talks, delivered by male speakers with backgrounds in business and leadership, focus on topics like leadership, marriage, and family, often with spiritual elements or a direct gospel invitation. These one-hour gatherings require effort and planning but have been highly successful in reaching both Christian and pre-Christian men.

Second | Flip The Acquisition Funnel

Think outside the box. In sales and marketing, customer acquisition funnels are designed to transform potential interest into committed clients. However, applying this model in church contexts, especially with limited resources and a small men's team, is often impractical. Here's a different approach: focus on a smaller, more engaged group.

Fact About Small Group Explosion

Starting with a single small group, I cultivated a ministry of 480 men across 40 groups in just 9 months. This was a revelation even after 20 years in ministry. Why are we surprised? Jesus's ministry grew using a similar approach.

For those with limited resources I recommend starting with a small, leadership-focused group. Find your most capable Christian man and have him lead a group focused on mentorship, discipleship, and leadership. This method may seem slower but is well-suited for volunteer-led teams with limited budgets.

Third | Think Deploy, Not Retain

Focus on sending, not just gathering. The traditional approach to men's ministry might need a rethink. For example, trying to replicate the success of large-scale events like those of Promise Keepers isn't always effective in today's context.

Fact About Men in Church Activities:

> "Midweek activities often draw 70 to 80 percent female participants." (Barna Research Online, "Women are the Backbone of Christian Congregations in America")

Since men are generally busy with work and other commitments, we should meet them where they are, helping them excel in their personal and professional lives with God's truth. Deploying men into various roles, whether it's leading family devotions, serving in church ministries, or mentoring in their workplaces can be more impactful than traditional gathering events. This approach is about empowering men to serve God's mission, not just retaining them within the church.

Our ministry, Resolute, focuses on this concept of deployment. We aim to disciple and develop men in a way that supports pastors and church leaders, encouraging men to take active leadership roles in their communities and workplaces.

In conclusion, building an effective men's ministry requires understanding the unique challenges and opportunities in engaging men. By adapting our strategies, focusing on smaller, more intentional groups, and deploying men into active service, we can create a more vibrant and effective ministry for men.

5 PROPOSALS THAT CULTIVATE BIBLICAL MANHOOD IN YOUR CHURCH

In a time where the very fabric of biblical manhood is being challenged and often undervalued, the urgency for the church to rise and reaffirm its commitment to cultivating true, scriptural male leadership has never been greater. This is not just a fleeting concern but a pressing issue that strikes at the heart of the church's ability to thrive and effectively fulfill its mission. The question that looms large is: how can the church not only navigate but also positively shape the landscape of gender roles and leadership in a way that honors God's original design?

Each proposal is a clarion call, urging us to look closely at the state of male leadership within our congregations and to take decisive, biblically grounded action. These are not mere suggestions but pivotal steps towards reclaiming and nurturing the essence of biblical manhood in a world increasingly drifting away from these fundamental truths.

One | Affirm Biblical Manhood: As leaders, our duty is to articulate the magnificence of biblical manhood with unwavering conviction. The scriptures provide a clear blueprint for male leadership. This is not a topic to be trivialized or shied away from. When we diminish or mock God's design for gender roles, we risk eroding the very essence of manhood as depicted in the Bible. It's imperative that we uphold these teachings with the gravity they deserve, avoiding the pitfalls of undermining God's ordained structure in our congregations.

Two | Present Authoritative Teaching That Speaks to Men: We must faithfully teach and preach the Scriptures, embracing its challenging truths. Men thirst for a word spoken with authority; tepid preaching leads to tepid lives. We need to inspire men with bold, convicting messages that call them to substantial commitment and action. Men are drawn to stories of bravery, sacrifice, and heroism – let's fuel this yearning by presenting them with a vision of life marked by selfless service, steadfast leadership, and unwavering devotion to Christ's kingdom.

Three | Clarity in Gender Roles: It's crucial to stand for a crystal-clear understanding of gender roles within our churches. This clarity should be evident in both practice and policy. We must resist the temptation to distort scriptural teachings through semantic gymnastics. If a role is pastoral in nature, altering titles does not rectify theological inaccuracies. Our focus should be on delineating the roles men are called to fulfill, emphasizing biblical complementarity not as a limitation for women but as a call to action for men.

Four | Foster Distinctive Gender Identities: From the earliest age, it is vital to nurture distinct gender identities intentionally. This doesn't imply segregation but rather a deliberate effort to guide boys toward biblical manhood and girls towards biblical womanhood, in line with Jesus' affirmation of God's creation: "Male and female, He created them."

Five | Empower Men for Leadership: We must proactively engage, train, and enable men for leadership roles within our churches. The foundation of church leadership and life is undeniably rooted in biblical manhood. A common challenge to male leadership in churches is the perceived scarcity of biblically qualified men for these roles. Our responsibility is to address this gap by actively preparing men for such vital positions.

Let us be steadfast in our resolve, recognizing that the journey to cultivate biblical manhood within the church is vital and transformative. This is not merely a call to action but a profound responsibility to uphold the scriptural truths that anchor our faith. By embracing these steps, we are not just fortifying the role of men in the church; we are contributing to a legacy of strong, godly leadership that will resonate through generations. Let us move forward with prayerful determination, guided by the Holy Spirit, to foster a community where biblical manhood is celebrated and lived out in its whole, God-honoring potential.

WHY MEN HAVE TROUBLE OPENING UP (AND WHAT TO DO)

Lack of transparency in a group is a classic challenge that must be overcome. Real transformation in a man's life will only happen when we go a little deeper by opening up and sharing more. From my experience, mature men and those who are spiritual leaders can invite this. They are willing to embrace their strengths, weaknesses, and uncertainties at a character level and have no problem sharing these – and some are even good at poking fun at themselves.

But this leaves us with two big questions:
1. First, why don't men open up?
2. Second, how do we get them to open up?

Why Men Have Trouble Opening Up

First | Men buy into the macho lie.

Men may not be aware of this, but slowly over a lifetime, we do buy into the macho lie. From a young age we blindly accept philosophical lies, delivered to us in anecdotal statements like "stop being a baby" and "don't act like a girl." These ideologies then get embedded into our thoughts, beliefs, and attitudes, and before we know it, we are passing them on to our children. Men have a skewed view of manhood.

Second | Men have not experienced healthy intimacy.

Many men have never experienced healthy intimacy with other men or women. I know that the word "intimacy" feels a little feminine to most men, but it's not. This is what all men want: to know and be known. In my childhood, I never had a healthy relationship with another man until my grandfather stepped in. And it took me years to push through this challenge. It was not until after college and marriage that I learned some of my first lessons about healthy versions of relationships and intimacy. Most men know what I am talking about. Even today, wrong understandings of intimacy still affect me in my relationship with my wife. But my wife has slowly, over the last 30 years, pushed me to share my feelings, care more about hers, and has got me to open up. And while we may think this is less than masculine, a real man is willing to be open and is not fearful of who is or what others think about it.

Third | Men need a safe place, and sometimes groups are not safe.

I hate this one, but it's the truth. Sometimes a men's small group in a church is not a safe and confidential environment. I know numerous men who avoid them for this reason. I hate that this prohibits them because we all want the best experience for our men and groups. The unfortunate outcome of this is that men who want community join a group and never go any deeper. They maintain surface-level depth and never get beyond facts and opinions to discover the amazement of transparency in a safe environment.

Fourth | Men have not experienced the incredible benefits of brotherhood.

There are all kinds of benefits of brotherhood. One is that when we become transparent, we can find ways to navigate and overcome the obstacles of life that keep tripping us up. Just take Alcoholics Anonymous, where men are forced to look inward, face their issues, and therefore witness the benefits of transparency in community with other men. Men who have never pushed through this miss profiting from the benefits of opening up. I think the 12 disciples experienced the benefits of this more than we realize because they were in each other's lives seven days a week and almost 24 hours every day. They were forced into intimacy and could not hide from each other or Jesus, and in doing so, they became incredible men who changed the world.

Fifth | Men have too much to hide.

There are men in your group who are hiding things. When I sit in a group of men, I always assume men are hiding things. For example, if facts show that five out of ten men are addicted to pornography and no one is talking about the issue in your group, then half the men hiding and lying. This is because men either like their sins or are ashamed of their sins. Therefore, they feel safer when they pretend to be the man rather than become the man that God wants them to be.

Sixth | Men don't know themselves well.

Often, men know a lot about sports, work, leadership, politics, and even religion but lack knowledge about themselves. Spiritual knowing is another level of knowledge. It is not information about but intimacy with. For us to be truly intimate with God, we must know the truth about ourselves and the depth of our sin. Some men have not genuinely discovered this, and sometimes pointing this out drives them further away.

So what can we do? How can we respond?

I have found some solutions over the years. And from experience, I can tell you that they work, especially in a small group environment.

Response #1 | Redefine Godly Manhood – overcome the macho lie.

You must redefine godly manhood for men. Jesus was the ultimate man from God's perspective. While Jesus does not look or act like Rambo, the Gladiator, or James Bond, he is the man that we should be modeling our life after.

Response #2 | Commit To A Long-Term Group – and teach healthy intimacy over time.

Long-term commitment works. Men who commit longer to a group will traverse the issues and challenges of intimacy together. If they do make a longer-term commitment, they will discover new levels of intimacy.

Response #3 | Meet One-On-One With Men – and bring a safe place to them.

For men who are not opening up, I buy them coffee and invite them into greater vulnerability. When they share with men, I often invite them to share these vulnerabilities with the group. It gives them a push and even a leadership role in the group for a session.

Response #4 | Thank Men When They Are Transparent – show the benefits to other men.

There is nothing that reinforces transparency better than rewarding the guys who are and do, because this teaches the other men how. Thank your men when they open up and you will discover the group culture will catch on and learn transparency is acceptable and safe.

Response #5 | Have Men Share Testimonies – and bring them out of hiding.

Testimonies are an excellent way to get men to open up and let men discover each other. After they are done, let other men ask them a few questions and watch group intimacy grow.

Response #6 | Dig Out Sin and Discuss Why – and help them to discover themselves.

I think the statement "Tell me more" is one of the best ways to get men to take a conversation deeper. As men share more, they also have time to reflect on themselves and the triggers and challenges they face.

We all have issues, and we all need to open up more, so why not take the first step and share a little more transparently with another man. And you don't have to call it intimacy! Call it something else. Call it seeking advice. Call it asking for help. Call it talking out a problem, but don't do nothing. Be the first to take the leap and see what God does.

THE CASE FOR MENTORING MEN IN YOUR CHURCH

In the journey of faith, the role of mentorship cannot be overstated, especially when it comes to guiding men in their spiritual walk. Why is this so crucial? Let's delve into four key reasons.

First | Men Crave Spiritual Mentorship

At the core, men are seekers of direction and purpose, longing for spiritual mentorship to navigate life's complexities. In our churches today there's a palpable thirst for wisdom that transcends mere knowledge. Men are seeking a deeper, more meaningful connection with their faith. This yearning for spiritual mentorship is not just about learning the ropes; it's about finding someone who can guide them in applying their faith in real-world scenarios. It's about integrating faith into every aspect of life, from family to work and beyond.

Second | The Challenge of Voicing the Need

Despite this deep-seated desire for guidance, many men struggle to articulate their need for mentorship. In a culture that often equates vulnerability with weakness, it's challenging for men to step forward and admit their need for help. This silent struggle is a barrier that many men face, leaving them isolated in their spiritual journey. It's essential for the church to recognize this hurdle and proactively offer avenues for men to connect with mentors without the fear of judgment or shame.

Third | The Dilemma of Whom to Ask

Even when men overcome the challenge of acknowledging their need for mentorship, another question looms: who do they turn to? The church is filled with potential mentors, but not all are equipped or prepared to take on this vital role. Men often seek someone who doesn't just share knowledge but also life experiences, someone who has walked the path they are on and has navigated the same challenges they face. Identifying these mentors within the church can be a daunting task for men who are already hesitant to seek help.

Fourth | The Need for Experienced Guidance

Men need mentors who have been down their road, who can empathize with their struggles and offer wisdom born of experience. It's not just about finding a guide; it's about finding the right guide. A mentor who has weathered life's storms and who can share both their victories and their failures becomes an invaluable resource for spiritual growth and personal development. These mentors serve not only as teachers but as living examples of how to walk faithfully through life's ups and downs.

The need for mentoring men in our churches is clear. It's a call to action for those who have walked the path of faith to step up and guide those who are navigating it. It's an opportunity to foster a community where men can grow, not just in knowledge, but in wisdom and character. As we embrace this call, we build not just better men but stronger churches and communities. Let us then commit to this vital mission, to mentor and be mentored, in our shared journey of faith.

GUIDING MEN FROM SHAME TO GRACE TO FREEDOM

You will encounter men in your ministry who are burdened by shame. Men who believe in Jesus yet often find themselves battling with the heavy burden of shame. This shame, deeply ingrained, can be a formidable barrier to drawing closer to God and fully engaging in his work.

The past actions, thoughts, and experiences that men have often fall short of God's standards. This recognition can give rise to a voice within men, declaring, 'God cannot utilize someone like me!' Some may even find themselves hesitating to approach Him, held back by the conviction that they are unworthy of His presence—a notion that, within our human understanding, may appear justifiable.

Navigating Through the Maze of Shame

Shame, in its essence, is a conviction of unworthiness. It arises from actions we regret, thoughts that trouble us, circumstances that challenge our sense of self-worth, or past experiences that have left deep scars. As believing men, we might find ourselves grappling with shame from various aspects of life, be it personal failures, struggles with temptations, or life's unexpected turns like job loss or relationship breakdowns.

What amplifies this shame is the enemy's persistence in reminding us of our flaws and failings. This relentless whisper can prevent us from establishing a more robust and intimate connection with God, as we become convinced of our undeservedness.

Experiencing the Transformative Power of Grace

In stark contrast to the despair of shame stands the radiant beacon of grace. Yes, it is true that by our measures, we fall short of God's glory. Yet grace unfolds the beautiful narrative of God's love - "While we were still sinners, Christ died for us" (Romans 5:8). This profound truth reveals that despite our unworthiness, God chose to redeem us through His sacrifice. Grace is not about our merit but about God's boundless mercy and love.

As believing men, understanding and accepting this grace is pivotal. It reassures us that our value in God's eyes is not based on our perfection but on His endless compassion. This grace is our lifeline, pulling us out of the depths of shame and into the embrace of God's love.

Point Men to True Freedom in Christ

Jesus Christ came to liberate us, to offer life in its fullest form. He came to release us from the chains of shame and unworthiness, and to initiate us into a life transformed by His Spirit. This freedom is in stark opposition to the enemy's strategy, which aims to steal our joy, suppress our freedom, and mire us in continuous feelings of inadequacy.

Remember this vital truth: if you are in a relationship with God, He has already lifted the burden of your shame and handled your sin. You are now free to walk in a life of liberty and deep communion with Him, ready to undertake the noble tasks He has set before you (Ephesians 2:10-11).

To all believing men, I urge you to reject the shackles of shame and embrace the freedom that Christ has secured for you. Dive into the scriptures, especially Ephesians chapters one and two, to understand how God perceives you now: redeemed, cherished, and empowered.

A Call to Action for Believing Men

The journey to overcoming shame and living in freedom requires intentional steps:

One | Recognize the Lie of Shame

Understand that shame is a tool used by the enemy to divert you from God's path. It's not a reflection of your true identity in Christ.

Two | Embrace the Truth of God's Word

Let the scriptures renew your mind. You are not what your past says; you are what God says - a redeemed and beloved son.

Three | Live in the Liberty of Christ

Step out of your past and into the identity Christ has given you. Engage actively in the life and works God has prepared for you.

In conclusion, let us not be hindered by the weight of shame, and let's guide other men from the same burden. Instead, together we should embrace the grace and freedom offered through Christ. This shift will lead to a deeper relationship with God, a life marked by purpose, and the joy of serving Him.

Remember, you are not defined by your failures but by God's unending grace and love. Stand firm in this truth today and every day.

7 CHARACTER CHALLENGES MEN ENCOUNTER

As you guide and mentor men in their walk with Christ, it's vital to recognize and address seven core challenges that shape our walk with the Lord. Our culture often leans towards apathy, avoiding responsibilities, and self-centeredness. As leaders, it's our duty to guide men towards embodying Christ's character. Remember, we're not just imparting knowledge; we're sculpting lives and characters.

Challenge One: Reject Passivity

In today's world, where silence or avoidance might seem like safe strategies, they're not fitting for a Christian man. Such approaches might offer temporary comfort but lead to long-term dissatisfaction. True strength lies in active engagement and decision-making, not in passivity.

Challenge Two: Accept Responsibility

The biblical principle of responsibility is starkly contrasted by instances in history, like President Clinton's infamous denial in 1998, which later proved false. Such moments highlight the importance of owning up to our actions and words, a crucial step in Christian maturity.

Challenge Three: Lead Courageously

Leadership requires a blend of courage, wisdom, and humility. As God commanded Joshua to be strong and courageous, so are we called to lead in various aspects of life. Courage isn't just about bold actions; it's also about wise listening and understanding when to act and when to step back.

Challenge Four: Love Eternally

God's love, showcased in 1 John 4:7 and through the life of Jesus Christ, sets the standard for how we should love. It's a love that goes beyond our human limitations and reflects God's eternal nature. As Christian men, we're called to emulate this love in all our relationships.

Challenge Five: Live With Integrity

Integrity is about aligning our actions with God's design and purpose for our lives. It's more than just keeping promises; it's about living in a way that fulfills the Creator's intent for us, reflecting His truth and justice in our everyday actions.

Challenge Six: Serve Humbly

True leadership involves serving others without ego or arrogance. As we develop skills and expertise, it's important to remember that our talents are gifts from God, meant to be used for serving others, not for self-promotion. Humility is key in godly service.

Challenge Seven: Invest Eternally

In a world obsessed with material wealth, we're called to invest in what lasts forever – our spiritual growth, relationships, and service to God. These eternal investments yield returns that far surpass any worldly gain, providing true satisfaction and purpose.

As we face these challenges, let's embrace them with faith, understanding that through them, we grow closer to Christ and become better leaders in His kingdom.

CALLING MEN INTO AN ADVENTUROUS FAITH

Living a life of faith is an adventure that transcends mere belief in Christ, regular church attendance, and biblical knowledge. It's about the bold willingness to follow Jesus into the unknown, to heed His commands, and to trust Him with our lives, especially when the path seems perilous and strays from our conventional understanding. This call to live a dangerous faith is not just about personal spiritual growth; it's a clarion call to those who mentor others, encouraging men to lead by example in this adventurous journey of faith.

Responding to God's Promptings: A Leap of Faith

Consider Abraham, a paragon of faith. When God called him to leave Ur for an unspecified land, Abraham didn't have modern navigational aids. What he had was far more profound-a steadfast faith in God. This act of blind obedience exemplifies the essence of a life of faith. It's about saying, "I will follow," even when the path is obscured by risks and fears. This is the faith of a mentor who guides others, not by certainty of the destination but by the certainty of God's character.

Choosing God's Way: The Radical Path of Obedience

True faith is more than an intellectual exercise in scriptural knowledge. It's about the practical application of God's Word. I admire men who not only know Scripture but live it, choosing God's directives over their personal preferences. This radical obedience, especially when it contradicts worldly logic, exemplifies a life of dangerous faith. For mentors, this means leading not just through words but through actions that reflect an unwavering commitment to God's path.

The Adventure of Living Dangerously: Embracing God's Call

Men are inherently drawn to adventure and challenge. God, in His infinite wisdom, calls us to a life that satisfies this intrinsic need-a life of faith on the edge. Imagine the thrill of living in alignment with a God who calls us to audacious endeavors, equipping us with the necessary strength and wisdom. This is not a passive faith; it's active, engaging, and exhilarating.

A Life-Changing Mantra from Proverbs

Proverbs 3:5-7 offers a powerful mantra for living a dangerous faith: "Trust in the Lord with all your heart and lean not on your own understanding; in all your ways submit to him, and he will make your paths straight. Do not be wise in your own eyes; fear the Lord and shun evil." This Scripture encapsulates the essence of a faith that challenges and changes us, promising spiritual health and vitality.

The Challenge to Both Mentors and Mentees

The question for every mentor and their mentee is this: Where is God calling you today to an adventure of faith? It's an invitation to step out of your comfort zone, embrace the unknown, and lead others in this thrilling journey of faith. The call to live a dangerous faith is not just about personal growth; it's about inspiring others to join this extraordinary adventure. Are you ready to take up this challenge and lead others into the exhilarating unknown of a life fully entrusted to God?

SECTION 2

MENTORSHIP & DISCIPLESHIP

3 MARKS: THAT WILL ACCELERATE MEN & YOUR MINISTRY TO MEN

I want you to reflect momentarily on a man (or men) who have shaped your life. Consider how they shaped and influenced you.

Are you thinking about them?

If so, you probably realize that you still long for that connection. Relationships that transcend the superficial and mundane. Relationships where we can be ourselves, be understood, and be challenged. But these relationships are far too scarce. We don't need many of these relationships, but men undeniably require a few solid spiritual bonds in their lives.

Here are three hallmarks of the strong bonds we should have with other men and that we want other men to find as well:

Mark One | Acceptance

Accept one another, then, just as Christ accepted you, in order to bring praise to God. — Romans 15:7

Men long for acceptance. But not just any acceptance. True biblical acceptance. There is a vast difference between the generalized acceptance that most think this verse is talking about.

Wrong acceptance is settling for a compromise that goes against biblical truth. It is a form of approval that condones sin or embraces ideologies that go against the teachings of Scripture. As advocated for here, proper acceptance is based on thoughtful discernment and spoken love. It involves accepting others, regardless of their flaws or past, while upholding God's truth and moral standards. Proper acceptance recognizes the inherent worth of a man as God's creation (Genesis 1:27) and acknowledges the need for repentance and transformation, which means we must get aligned with God's truth (Acts 3:19).

This is the kind of acceptance that marks great masculine relationships. It says, "I love you, man, but I don't want you to repeat the same mistakes. I want you to be a better man. A more godly man." We must be that man and guide men to other men who will do the same.

Mark Two | Truth

Instead, speaking the truth in love, we will grow to become in every respect the mature body of him who is the head, that is, Christ.
— Ephesians 4:15

Men also need another man who will speak the truth to them. But the basis for this truth does not stem from their opinions. It's founded on the only truth we have–scripture. And scripture has a caveat on how we speak it–we must speak it in love. It's truth with a purpose–spiritual growth and maturity. In other words, men need men who will speak biblical truth in loving ways to other men, so they will grow spiritually.

Plenty of men out there don't know how to do this. They might only speak their opinions. Or they might know the truth but only say it harshly. Or they speak it with no interest in helping others spiritually grow. And many men have been ruined by spiritual relationships that have done this all wrong—men who have failed in every aspect of this truth.

Here is a short list of aspirational targets for the man who is able to speak truth in love:
- He wants God's best for men.
- He understands the challenges of men.
- He speaks your language.
- He makes steps actionable.
- He gives constructive feedback.
- He remains committed to you.

Here's the deal: if you want to grow in the truth as a man of God, you must be willing to step into these moments. It's never easy or perfect. It will be messy sometimes. Men say stupid things in stupid ways because we are all a little stupid sometimes. But avoiding this mark is not the path to becoming a better man of God nor making men better.

Mark Three | Vulnerability

Bear one another's burdens, and so fulfill the law of Christ.
— Galatians 6:2

Iron sharpens iron, and one man sharpens another. — Proverbs 27:17

The final hallmark is the safety of being vulnerable. In these types of relationships, men can fully expose their true selves and confront their struggles without the fear of abandonment or rejection. This environment offers men security where they can lay bare their issues, confusion, and sin, knowing they will be met with compassion and understanding.

Most men have never experienced this. There are many reasons why, including social expectations, cultural norms, upbringing, and some unfortunate experiences with other men or Christian men. As a result, being vulnerable means first getting beyond all these hurts and hang-ups. And for some, this makes vulnerability daunting.

But true godly vulnerability is where men are made. When a vulnerable piece of metal is placed in the ironsmith's hands, he is subject to the ironsmith's discretion. And yes, there is heat, beating, and grinding. But if we subject ourselves to a vulnerable process, on the other side, shape, sharpening, and shining happen. But it only happens when we are vulnerable and submit ourselves to vulnerability. And this goes for both men in a relationship. We must model vulnerability and be vulnerable.

There are your three hallmarks: Acceptance. Truth. Vulnerability.

By embracing these we pave the way for authentic, transformative relationships that reflect the love of Christ. Remember, we must model these marks ourselves and seek out men who embody them. In doing so, you will experience the power and beauty of godly masculine relationships that shape and strengthen men on their path to becoming the man God has called you and them to be.

MENTORSHIP: THE CORNERSTONE OF BUILDING MEN IN FAITH

In today's world, where the concept of manhood is often muddled and misinterpreted, discipleship and mentorship emerge as crucial elements in guiding men toward a clear and faith-based understanding of masculinity. Here's how mentorship can play a pivotal role in shaping the character and faith of men in future generations.

9 Values of Mentorship

One | Guides Men Through the Crisis of Manhood: The modern world throws conflicting messages about what it means to be a man. Mentorship offers a haven to address these issues. Through discipleship, men can explore and define their identities, aligning them with biblical principles and a faith-centered view of manhood.

Two | Battles Isolation with Brotherhood: Many men face the challenge of isolation, often missing out on deep connections with their peers. Mentorship bridges this gap, fostering a sense of community and brotherhood. It's in these relationships that men find support and strength, particularly during tough times.

Three | Shares Wisdom Across Generations: Today's fast-paced societal changes highlight the importance of intergenerational relationships. Elder men bring wisdom and experience, while younger men contribute fresh ideas and energy. This synergy is vital for the health and growth of the church.

Four | Cultivates Future Leaders: The church thrives on strong leadership. Through mentorship, men are groomed with the skills, knowledge, and character necessary to lead. This preparation is key to the church's resilience and future growth.

Five | Fosters Spiritual Maturity: Discipleship is all about deepening one's faith and understanding of Scripture. Men rooted in their faith are more likely to embody Christ's teachings, positively influencing their families, workplaces, and communities.

Six | Models Christ-like Behavior: Christian mentorship is a practical way to demonstrate Christ-like behavior in everyday life. It provides a real-life example for men to follow, showing how faith can be lived out daily.

Seven | Guides Through Life's Challenges: Life is full of challenges and transitions. A mentor can be a guiding light, offering wisdom and faith-based advice. This support is invaluable for making decisions that align with faith and values.

Eight | Sustains Faith in a Secular World: In a world often dominated by secular views, maintaining strong faith is a challenge. Mentorship provides the necessary support and encouragement to keep faith alive and growing amidst external pressures.

Nine | Creates a Legacy of Faith: Mentorship allows men to pass down a legacy of faith to the next generation. This legacy is essential to ensure the ongoing strength and vitality of the church and its mission.

In summary, discipleship and mentorship are fundamental in nurturing strong, faith-filled men for future generations. These practices provide a comprehensive approach to spiritual growth, community building, and leadership development, ensuring that the church remains a dynamic and influential force in the lives of men and their communities.

ENLISTING OTHERS: THE COLLECTIVE EFFORT OF MEN'S MINISTRY

Extraordinary leadership, especially in the context of men's ministry, is a journey that transcends personal ambitions, focusing instead on nurturing and empowering others in their faith. This kind of leadership isn't about being the center of attention or having others follow you blindly. Rather, it's about inspiring men to subscribe to a vision that resonates deeply with them, a vision they can carry forward with or without your presence. In men's ministry this approach is crucial as it shifts the focus from individual ego to a collective mission in Christ.

Here are five principles of leadership tailored for men's ministry:

Principle One: Understanding the Choice of Followers

In men's ministry, leaders recognize that followers make a conscious decision to engage. You don't choose them; they choose you. This choice is often driven by two factors. First, you have articulated a vision - a godly, noble cause that speaks to their hearts. In the realm of spiritual leadership, it's essential to call men to a cause greater than themselves, one that serves God and His kingdom. Second, they follow because they see in you a man worth emulating. In a world where true role models are scarce, be a man of godly character and vision, and you will naturally attract followers.

Principle Two: Leading Through Persuasion

In men's ministry, leaders excel not by commanding but by persuading, leading with the heart of Christ. This distinction is vital. While secular leadership might tolerate directives, spiritual leadership thrives on inspiration and influence. Being persuasive in a godly manner means being passionate about Christ's mission, advocating for it, and aligning your character with His teachings. When you lead with integrity and a cause that honors God, men will be drawn to join you.

Principle Three: Investing in Fellow Men

Leadership in men's ministry is about investing in the spiritual growth and well-being of other men. It's a commitment to guide them towards fulfilling their God-given potential. As a steward of God's work, your focus should be on nurturing others so that the collective vision of your ministry is realized. This investment is about building up men in faith, so the ministry's goals are achieved, ideally reaching a point where the vision can thrive, even in your absence.

Principle Four: Demonstrating Competence in Spiritual Leadership

Competence is crucial, particularly in leading men towards spiritual growth. Your ability to guide, teach, and inspire is central to enlisting others in the ministry's vision. Leadership in men's ministry is a skill that demands continuous learning and spiritual growth. As Proverbs 27:17 says, "Iron sharpens iron, and one man sharpens another." Stay diligent in your personal and spiritual development to maintain the trust and respect of those you lead.

Principle Five: Exemplifying Godly Values and Character

A leader in men's ministry must embody the values and character of Christ. Integrity builds trust and encourages others to follow. Any deviation from these godly principles can lead to a loss of trust and followership. Therefore, prioritize your walk with God, ensuring your actions and decisions reflect His teachings. This approach not only strengthens your leadership but also sets a powerful example for the men in your ministry.

In conclusion, extraordinary leadership in men's ministry is about guiding men towards a shared, Christ-centered vision. It's a selfless journey where you serve as a catalyst, empowering others to grow in their faith and live out their God-given purpose. This leadership style calls for a heart devoted to Christ, an unwavering commitment to integrity, and a passion for nurturing and guiding fellow men in their spiritual journey.

TRAIN & PREPARE A WINGMAN

As we build ministry, the significance of having a faithful wingman cannot be overstated. The "wingman" concept, deeply rooted in military parlance, refers to a reliable companion who watches your back while you watch his. In ministry, this translates to a comrade-in-arms who shares your mission, your struggles, and your victories. But how do we train and prepare a wingman for everything we do in ministry? Let's dig into this, drawing from the wisdom of Scripture and years of practical experience.

One | Identify the Right Man

First and foremost, pray for discernment. The right wingman is someone who not only shares your faith but also your vision for ministry. This individual should be trustworthy, dependable, and ready to grow. Remember, Jonathan and David's relationship in the Bible? It was based on mutual respect, shared faith, and a commitment to God's plan (1 Samuel 18:1-4). Seek someone with a similar heart.

Two | Foster Mutual Reliance

In Proverbs 27:17 we read, "As iron sharpens iron, so one person sharpens another." Training your wingman involves creating an environment of mutual accountability. Be transparent with your struggles and encourage them to do the same. This accountability isn't just about correcting each other, but more about growing together in Christ.

Three | Equip Them with Knowledge, Modeling & Skills

Just as Paul mentored Timothy, take time to equip your wingman with the necessary knowledge and skills for ministry. This includes studying the Bible together, sharing resources, and involving them in your ministry activities. Remember, training is not just about imparting knowledge but also about developing character.

Four | Set an Example

Leadership is more caught than taught. Set an example in speech, in conduct, in love, in faith, and in purity (1 Timothy 4:12). Your life should be a living epistle, inspiring your wingman to emulate Christ in all aspects of life and ministry.

Five | Draw Out Their Gifts

Every individual is blessed with unique gifts (1 Corinthians 12:4-6). Encourage your wingman to identify and use their God-given talents in the service of the Kingdom. The body of Christ needs all its parts functioning effectively.

Six | Engage in Shared Missions

Take your wingman along in your ministry endeavors. Whether it's a mission trip, a Bible study group, or a community service project, let them experience the joys and challenges of ministry firsthand. This hands-on approach is invaluable for learning.

Seven | Pray Together

Emphasize the power and necessity of prayer. Pray with and for your wingman regularly. Encourage them to develop a robust personal prayer life. As you both seek God's guidance and strength, your bond in Christ will deepen.

Eight | Provide Constructive Feedback

Be honest in your feedback, always aiming to build up rather than tear down (Ephesians 4:29). Constructive feedback helps your wingman to grow in areas they may not see themselves.

Nine | Celebrate Milestones Together

Acknowledge and celebrate milestones in your ministry and personal growth. These moments of celebration reinforce the sense of team spirit and shared purpose.

Ten | Prepare for Multiplication

Finally, prepare your wingman to become a leader who will, in turn, train his wingman. The goal is to create a multiplying effect, expanding the reach of the Gospel.

We are not lone rangers. We need faithful wingmen who walk with us, fight with us, and keep us accountable. By training and preparing a wingman, we strengthen not only our ministry but also the broader body of Christ. In this sacred endeavor, let us always look to Jesus, the author, and perfecter of our faith, who exemplified the ultimate model of leadership and companionship.

4 TRAITS FOR BECOMING AN EFFECTIVE MENTOR & MEN'S LEADER

Embarking on the journey of mentoring another man, like desiring mentorship ourselves, requires understanding the qualities of an effective spiritual mentor. This exploration often raises the question, "What traits embody a great mentor?" Here we delve into four pivotal traits that define an exceptional spiritual mentor.

Trait One | A Disposition For Growth

The pursuit of spiritual growth is crucial, acknowledging that none of us have reached the pinnacle of our spiritual journey. This journey isn't about achieving perfection but about a steadfast commitment to growing closer to the image of Jesus Christ. A great mentor recognizes this and is open to feedback, ready to adapt and grow. Their passion for spiritual receptivity not only guides others towards Christ but also enriches their own faith journey. In mentoring, both the mentor and mentee evolve, learning invaluable lessons from each other.

Trait Two | A Relatable Leader

Relatability is key in mentorship. No one can connect with someone who claims perfection, as we all have our flaws. True mentorship involves sharing both triumphs and failures. It's through our struggles that we carve out our character, learning to embody virtues like courage and faith. A great mentor is transparent, sharing their life experiences, including their missteps, to guide others in their life journey. This openness fosters a genuine, honest relationship, crucial for effective mentorship.

Trait Three | A Developer of People

Mentoring is an honor, but it's vital to remember that our role isn't to mold our mentees in our image. God created each individual uniquely. The aim is not to replicate our beliefs or actions but to guide them towards becoming more like Christ, as is the essence of being a Christian and a disciple. This means teaching from the Word and modeling a life that strives to emulate Jesus, the master mentor.

Trait Four | A Curious Guide

A misconception in mentorship is the belief that mentors must always provide direct answers. However, a great mentor understands the value of asking insightful questions. This approach fosters critical thinking and guides mentees to seek God's direction in their lives. It's more about offering perspective and wisdom, encouraging engagement with the Scriptures and prayer, allowing the Holy Spirit to work in their lives. Just as Jesus often used questions to provoke thought, a great mentor excels in creating a dialogue that uncovers the best in others, knowing when to teach and when to inquire.

In sum, being a great spiritual mentor isn't about being perfect or having all the answers. It's about being committed to growth, sharing life honestly, guiding others towards Christ, and fostering thoughtful inquiry. These traits not only make for effective disciple-making but also contribute to the mentor's own spiritual growth and understanding.

MENTORS ASK THE BEST QUESTIONS

Let's discuss why mentors (and mentees) should all be asking better questions than knowing and giving the right answers. I have some friends who stand out as leaders and who have unknowingly mentored me through contact with them. One of their traits is that they are amazingly curious and always ask good, penetrating questions that cause me to think and reflect more deeply. I always leave our conversations feeling that they are interested in me and what I do, and the dialogue that comes out of their questions enriches me.

The art of asking good questions is often overlooked. Some people like to talk, and they talk a lot, usually about themselves and their accomplishments. Some merely listen, which is often better than talking, but the wisest are people who ask penetrating questions, listen carefully, and even think to ask follow-up questions.

So why is asking good questions a genius move by a mentor? Here is the genius, it becomes a mechanism of learning for both parties. Whether it is about business, personal matters, or family, the best way to understand another individual is to ask questions. Not only that, but those we are with often have a wealth of information that we didn't know, which adds to our knowledge and often triggers ideas for us in life and business.

It also helps both parties to think more deeply, and they often come to greater clarity as they answer. It deepens relationships even if they are new because questions invariably say, "I am interested in you, what you do, and what you think." Self-absorbed people tend to pontificate and talk while healthy individuals are inquisitive and focus on those around them. In fact, you can gauge the emotional health (EQ) of others by how many questions they ask.

Asking good questions is a skill we can all learn. Good question-asking is a learned skill for most of us, and if practiced, it can be developed. Here are some of the kinds of questions I have found that open up a conversation and lead to greater in-depth dialogue.

- Tell me about your work?
- What do you love about what you do?
- What is the most significant challenge in your job?
- How do you stay sharp, and what do you do to keep growing?
- What is your happiness factor from one to ten? What would make it higher?
- Tell me about your family?
- How did you end up doing what you currently do?
- How have you defined your purpose in life?
- What life circumstances have most defined who you are today?

You can see how questions like this can lead to a much broader conversation as well as cause others to reflect more deeply on their own life and work. Those you are with will also know that you care about them and are interested in them and who they are. If you want to be a person of influence and a great mentor, learn the art of asking great questions.

5 KEYS TO MENTORING RELATIONSHIPS

Throughout history, mentors have played a pivotal role in shaping godly men. When we turn to the Bible, we discover mentorship was the basis and the core practice from the beginning of the Bible. For example, consider Moses and Joshua, Elijah and Elisha, Paul and Timothy, and Jesus and his disciples. The power and effects of mentorship are undeniable and beneficial.

The Old Testament Law highlighted the importance of passing on wisdom and knowledge from generation to generation (Deuteronomy 6:4-9). Mentoring was the key. In the New Testament we see Jesus, who was easily the greatest mentor of all time. He handpicked twelve men and poured his heart and soul into them. Their lives were forever changed, and they went on to change the world. We are having this conversation because of Jesus's mentorship with twelve men. Therefore, when we step into the role of being a mentor and then actively and intentionally mentor another man, we become a partner in the ancient mission many have called the Great Commission.

Most men understand this. The problem they have is understanding what to do. Here is a framework for thinking about mentorship that will help you demystify the process and jump into the greatest mission godly men can ever participate in.

Let's break mentoring down into five essential keys:

Key One | Get Your Motives Right

Certain persons, by swerving from these, have wandered away into vain discussion, desiring to be teachers of the law, without understanding either what they are saying or the things about which they make confident assertions. — 1 Timothy 1:6-7

First things first. Before you can be an effective mentor, you must assess yourself. As Paul said to Timothy, you need to ensure that your motives are right. This is because some people get into mentorship for all the wrong reasons. Based on this text, if you are doing it for personal glory, you are doing it for the wrong reasons, which leads to pointless bloviating and inflated egos. And this is not why we mentor. So, if you are thinking about mentoring or discipling someone, are you doing it for the right reasons? And here is why this is important. You are not the mentor. Jesus is. Scripture is. The Spirit is. You are merely a humble follower leading another man into the same following. Don't blow this first step. If you get this wrong, all the other steps will be wrong because your motives impact everything.

Key Two | Get To Know The Mentees Motives & Obstacles

Now when Simon saw that the Spirit was given through the laying on of the [Peter and John's] hands, he offered them money, saying, "Give me this power also, so that anyone on whom I lay my hands may receive

the Holy Spirit . . . And Simon answered, "Pray for me to the Lord, that nothing of what you have said may come upon me."
— *Acts 8:18-19, 24*

In the book of Acts, we find a powerful illustration of the importance of understanding the motives and obstacles of those we mentor. It's the story of Simon, who witnessed the miraculous power of the Holy Spirit through the laying on of hands by Peter and John. Simon was so captivated by this supernatural display that he offered them money, hoping to obtain the same power.

Simon's initial motives were driven by the desire for power and recognition. He wanted to perform miracles like Peter and John, but his heart was not in the right place. It's a reminder that not all motives are pure, even when someone appears enthusiastic about spiritual matters.

As mentors, we often face the same challenge. We may encounter mentees who seem eager to grow spiritually, but like Simon, their motives may be mixed. They might seek recognition, validation, or even material gain. This is where our role as mentors becomes crucial.

A crucial aspect of effective mentorship is understanding your mentee. This is where most mentors experience initial concern that they won't have the knowledge, skills, or ability to help. But this is still the right place to begin. Only the mentee can reveal the best place to begin and where they need to grow.

The key here is to keep asking good questions. Invite them to express their spiritual aspirations, areas of challenge, and even a sin struggle. By actively listening, you'll gain valuable insights into wrong motives and desires and discover obstacles. This is the key. Recognizing the motives and obstacles that hold your mentee back is vital. These barriers come in various forms, such as self-doubt, fear, or sinful influences. By helping them identify these obstacles, you will, over time, drive them toward positive spiritual change.

So, like Simon, who eventually recognized the error of his motives and sought prayer, our mentees may need guidance and correction. Our role is not just to impart knowledge but to guide hearts toward a genuine, transformative relationship with God. By understanding their motives and obstacles, we can help them navigate the path to true spiritual growth.

Key Three | Aim At Goals Together

> *You have heard that it was said, "You shall not commit adultery."*
> *But I say to you that everyone who looks at a woman with lustful intent*
> *has already committed adultery with her in his heart.*
> *— Matthew 5:27-28*

I love that Jesus tells us to rethink our spiritual goals. He tells us our goals need to be set on the right goal. He does this repeatedly through the Sermon on the Mount. But remember, goal setting is not the goal. The goal is to be like Jesus, which is impossible without the Spirit of God. But setting goals helps us to take steps in the right direction. Goals mentor us, but they don't make us. Therefore, we have to set goals with a mentee. We should do this with them. It helps men make tangible what is often intangible and abstract. Remember, you can set a goal of being more spiritually mature, but this will never be tangible enough for another man unless you make it measurable. First, I would encourage your mentee to identify one specific goal they want to achieve. Make sure it is specific, measurable, achievable, relevant, and time-bound — SMART, if you will. And then keep this goal front-and-center until they have made specific progress on it. I promise doing this together is worth the time, and the outcomes you both experience are much better.

Key Four | Focus on Behaviors and Skills

> *Know this, my beloved brothers: let every person be quick to hear, slow to speak, slow to anger; for the anger of man does not produce the righteousness of God.* — *James 1:19-20*

I love the letter of James. It's practical, and men like practicality because they respond to being told what to do. This verse is a good example. Be quick once. Be slow twice. I can understand that. So get practical. Recommend avoiding negative behaviors and then recommend positive behaviors, routines, and habits to embrace. Make sure they know how to do it. Give them the skills they need to overcome challenges. Encourage them to try a new behavior and adjust as needed so they will form new patterns. And keep adjusting it till the behavior becomes unconscious to them.

Key Five | Hold Them Accountable

Accountability is a part of the secret sauce to formalized mentorship. Regular check-ins, updated direction, and spiritual support are critical components. Hold them accountable at the top of the next meeting and listen to how they respond. Celebrate their wins and help them bounce back from setbacks. Just being there is critical.

Five keys. But remember, mentorship is always a two-way street. While you will guide and inspire another man, you'll grow along the way, too. Step in and discover the incredible high-speed growth potential of two men intentionally doing life together. It's a powerful combination.

6 STEPS TO FINDING A MENTOR & 3 TYPES OF MENTORS

How can a man build a mentoring relationship and forge a plan for a better future?

While we often aspire to be better men, aspiration will not be enough. We must build a better plan to become a better man. The following are six steps to consider helping you develop an effective plan. (Hint: Consider utilizing the questions for developing your plan.)

First | Take A Personal Inventory

As a mentee, there are some things that only we can define. We need to take inventory and identify your goals, the challenges, and the assets at your disposal. While I have started mentoring relationships without these, at some point, these come into play and will undermine your attitude in the relationship if they are not being met. Taking a personal inventory is our responsibility, not the mentor. So, we must put pen to paper and define our goals, challenges, and assets.

Questions to consider:
- What goals do you want to accomplish?

- What challenges do you face and anticipate facing in accomplishing these goals?
- What assets do you have and need to accomplish your goals?

Second | Consider the Vision, Goals, and Outcomes

As men, we need to spend some time developing our vision. Vision is our picture of the future; in this case, it is who we aspire to be. This activity is summarized in us articulating the man God designed you to be and identifying the goals and outcomes for living in this vision. We will be drawn to specific goals and outcomes as we consider our personal vision, but enumerating and stating them is harder than we think.

Here is an example of a goal I have set in the past.

"This year, I want to learn to eat and live healthier to increase my skill and stamina for kingdom leadership."

- The vision is kingdom leadership.
- The goal is to learn to eat and live healthier.
- The outcomes are increased skill and stamina.

Questions to consider:
- What vision do you want to accomplish as a man of God?
- What goals do you need to establish to get there?
- What outcomes do you expect?

Third | Determine Relational Scope

While we will need mentors for our lifetime, we are not sentencing a mentor for life. Therefore, we need to decide the meeting time frame, length of commitment, and frequency of meetings in the mentor relationship that would be the best win-win for both parties. Clearly, each mentor will have different levels of accessibility, so consider the scope, which is dependent on the mentor's availability.

Questions to consider:
- What is the time frame of each meeting that is best for them and me?
- What length of commitment is best for them and me?
- What frequency of meeting is best for them and me?

Fourth | Identify The Type Of Mentor You Need

We cannot go through life alone, but many men do, so I think we can get stuck at this step. But this can be a hurdle only if we do not know what type of mentor we seek. Three general types of mentors can help, and we can have any one or even all three at the same time. It is good to know what we need based on how we have answered any or all the above questions.

The three types of mentors:
- **Intensive Mentors** – This mentor is focused on our vision, goals, and outcomes and is in regular contact with us. They set up a structure and routine for a meeting. There is sometimes even live feedback and real-time interaction, which requires visibility of your performance behaviors.

- **Intermittent Mentors** – This is a non-formal type of mentor who, like a counselor, helps to guide us intermittently around a particular subject matter. There often is no real regular rhythm to a meeting until a need presents itself. Therefore, meetings and communication are more spontaneous.
- **Instructive Mentors** – This is the type of mentor who we may admire but never contact. We learn from them, but they will not know us. For example, authors and speakers would fit this category. We will have regular contact with their resources, but it is a one-way or passive process.

Questions to consider:
- What type of mentor do you need?
- Do you need more than one type of mentor, and if so, which ones?

Five | Determine Accountability Metrics

While we have established the goals above, how accountability occurs is critical. Our willingness to be accountable is essential to success, and only we know our desire. Often this has a direct correlation to how dedicated we are in accomplishing our goals. In other words, the more willing we are to become better, the more willing we are to be held accountable. And the opposite is also true, and so this is where the rubber meets the road.

Questions to consider:
- Are you willing to be held accountable?
- How badly do you want to accomplish your goals?
- What type of accountability do you need to reach your goals?

Six | Create Good Communication

Finally, we must determine how we will communicate in the mentor relationship. While this might feel like an add-on to this list, it is not. We need two things in communication. One is honesty with transparency. Two, we need to determine the best modes of communication between meetings, which keep the connection vibrant and active.

Questions to consider:
- What level of transparency do you need to be effective?
- How often will you communicate between meetings?

THE GRADUAL RELEASE MODEL: A JOURNEY FOR MENTORING & LEADING

Spiritual mentoring is like to a sacred pilgrimage, one that we undertake not in isolation but in relationship with others. In this journey, there are four pivotal yet interconnected stages, each marking a significant milestone in the shared growth of both the mentor and the mentee. These stages form what is called among educators the "Gradual Release Model," a process that beautifully mirrors the evolution of spiritual maturity and leadership.

I Do, You Watch:

This stage is foundational. As a mentor, you are the trailblazer, setting an example in spiritual disciplines and practices. It's about living out your faith authentically and wholeheartedly, demonstrating the essence of a Christ-centered life. Your mentee watches, not just to replicate your actions but to grasp the deeper values and convictions that drive them. This stage is less about instruction and more about inspiration, as you model a life of faith, integrity, and devotion.

I Do, You Help:

Here, the dynamic starts to shift. The mentee, having observed and absorbed, begins to partake in the spiritual journey more actively. While you, as the mentor, continue to lead and set the path, the mentee steps in to assist. This could be through participating in ministry activities, joining in prayer, or engaging in biblical discussions. This stage is crucial because it allows the mentee to apply what they've learned in a supportive environment, fostering a sense of involvement, and belonging in their spiritual walk.

You Do, I Help:

This stage is pivotal. The mentee emerges from the wings to take center stage. As a mentor, your role transforms from leader to supporter. The mentee now leads in spiritual endeavors, be it leading a prayer, facilitating a bible study, or engaging in ministry work. Your role is to guide, encourage, and offer wisdom. This stage is where confidence and skill in the mentee bloom, nurtured by your steady support and faith in their abilities.

You Do, I Watch:

The culmination of the journey. In this final stage, the mentee steps fully into their spiritual leadership. As a mentor, you observe, available for counsel and feedback but largely in a role of quiet support. It's a moment of profound joy and fulfillment, seeing the mentee equipped, empowered, and soaring in their faith journey. This stage symbolizes the successful transfer of spiritual leadership, where the mentee is now ready to embark on their own mentoring journey.

THE GRADUAL RELEASE MODEL: A JOURNEY FOR MENTORING & LEADING

This model isn't just a method; it's a manifestation of discipleship as modeled by Christ. It reflects the essence of biblical mentorship-a process of growth, empowerment, and multiplication of faith leaders. In every stage, there's shared growth, mutual learning, and an ever-deepening bond forged in the fires of faith. As mentors, we're called not just to lead but to eventually step back and watch as our mentees become leaders. It's a journey that requires patience, humility, and an unwavering commitment to the growth of those we mentor. In doing so, we don't just grow individuals; we expand the Kingdom of God.

THE FRAMEWORK OF SPIRITUAL MENTORING: STRUCTURING THE EXPERIENCE

To navigate this journey effectively, a framework is essential. This framework isn't rigid; it's a flexible guide, allowing each mentoring relationship to grow organically while maintaining direction and purpose.

First | Pick Your Win:
- Identify Your Strengths: As a mentor, what unique skills and experiences do you bring? These are your tools for building into another's life.
- Understand the Need: What are your mentee's spiritual needs and goals? Aligning your strengths to these needs is critical.
- Set Boundaries: Know what you're not willing to do. This protects both you and your mentee and ensures a healthy mentoring relationship.

- Seek Mutual Benefit: Consider how both can grow. Is there room for reverse mentoring, where you also learn from your mentee?

Second | Decide the Frequency:

- Determine Duration: Agree on a time frame, typically between 3 to 9 months, allowing for substantial growth without feeling overwhelmed.
- Set Meeting Rhythms: How often will you meet? Regularity breeds consistency and depth.
- Establish Communication Norms: What's the best way to keep in touch outside of meetings? Decide on the frequency and mode of communication.

Third | Select How You Will Monitor:

- Define Accountability: What will accountability look like in your relationship? It's not just about checking boxes but ensuring meaningful progress.
- Set Interim Goals: What should be accomplished between meetings? Small, achievable goals keep the momentum going.
- Commit to Confidentiality: Trust is the bedrock of any mentoring relationship. Agree on the level of confidentiality to maintain a safe space for open sharing.
- Outline Goals and Outcomes: Establish 1-3 overarching goals for your time together. These guide your journey

and provide a clear vision of success.

Embracing the Mentor's Heart

In spiritual mentoring, it's not just about what you do; it's about who you are. As mentors, we're called to exhibit Christ-like humility, patience, and love. Our goal is not to create copies of ourselves but to foster an environment where mentees can grow into the unique individuals God designed them to be.

Remember, every man we mentor is on his own spiritual journey. Our role is to walk alongside them, offering guidance, wisdom, and support as they discover their path. We're not just imparting knowledge; we're shaping lives. This requires an attentive ear, a discerning spirit, and a heart that genuinely seeks their best.

The Ripple Effect of Spiritual Mentoring

The impact of spiritual mentoring extends far beyond the immediate relationship. It's a ripple effect. The men we mentor today will, in turn, become mentors themselves, perpetuating a cycle of spiritual growth and leadership. This is how we build a legacy, one life at a time.

So, as we embark on this sacred journey of spiritual mentoring let's do so with intentionality, humility, and a deep sense of purpose. Our investment has the power to transform lives, not just for the present but for eternity. Let's cultivate mastery in this art of guidance, shaping the future one man, one soul, at a time.

THE K.M.S. MINDSET FOR MENTORING & BUILDING MEN

As leaders step into the vital role of guiding and mentoring others, they embark on a profound journey of transformation and discipleship. In this journey, three fundamental pillars—Knowledge, Modeling, and Skills, collectively known as the KMS mindset—take center stage, echoing the very principles that Jesus lived out with his own disciples. These pillars form the blueprint for effective mentoring and are indispensable in shaping men into the strong and faithful individuals they are called to be. Let's delve deeper into this transformative framework and explore how it can revolutionize the way we mentor and build men. Here is the breakdown.

Knowledge – What men need to know.

Knowledge helps us gain new insights and perspectives (or reminds us of them) through teaching, discussion, and observation.

Here are some things men need to know:
- **Biblical Foundations:** A strong understanding of the whole bible, including key scriptures, stories, and theological concepts.

- **Doctrine:** It's important for men to grasp the core doctrines of the Christian faith, such as the Trinity, salvation, sin, and grace, which form the bedrock of their beliefs.
- **Ancient & Christian History:** Teaching men about the history of the Christian church, its early leaders, and significant events can provide context and perspective on the faith's journey through the ages.
- **Apologetics:** Equipping men with the ability to defend their faith and engage in meaningful conversations about Christianity with others is crucial in today's world.
- **Practical Wisdom:** Knowledge isn't just theoretical; it's also about understanding how biblical principles apply to everyday life. This includes topics like marriage, parenting, work ethics, and finances from a Christian perspective.
- **Cultural Issues:** Helping men navigate the challenges and questions posed by contemporary culture and societal issues in light of their faith is essential.
- **Spiritual Disciplines:** Teach men the importance of spiritual practices such as prayer, meditation, fasting, and studying the Word. Show them how to integrate these disciplines into their daily routines.

Remember, knowledge is the foundation upon which everything else is built. Providing men with a solid biblical and doctrinal foundation equips them to make informed decisions, live out their faith, and become effective leaders and mentors themselves.

Modeling – What men need to see.

In modeling, the man learns by observing the leader or mentor. This may be something a leader shares from his life, how he interacts with others, or how he responds to situations. We need to think about character traits to be intentionally modeled.

Here are some examples:

- **Vulnerability:** Be open about your struggles. Model how you depend on God.
- **Ownership:** Be real about your issues. Model how you are dealing with your issues.
- **Reconcile:** Share relational conflicts. Model how you are pursuing peace in a conflict.
- **Wisdom:** Disclose decisions you are making. Model how God guided the decision-making process.

Skills – What men need to do.

Skills are areas that need hands-on training and the opportunity to ask questions to ensure that the individual can utilize the skill proficiently. There are a number of these areas in our lives as followers of Christ.

- **Spiritual Skills:** Spiritual practices like prayer and Bible reading are sometimes abstract activities where men need concrete direction.
- **Decision-Making Skill & Discernment:** Seeing things from a biblical worldview requires rethinking

how we handle conflict, anger, money, discipline, and even simple things like our words.

- **Leadership & Mentoring Skills:** In every phase and stage of life men are going to need specific skills. Being a husband, father, grandfather, leader, and mentor all require some level of skill. Pass the necessary skills onto them. Show them how to love, forgive, and extend grace.

In conclusion, the KMS mindset for mentoring and building men is a powerful framework that encapsulates the essence of discipleship, just as Jesus exemplified with his own disciples. Remember these three key elements: Knowledge, Modeling, and Skills. Through the diligent pursuit of knowledge, the intentional modeling of character traits, and the hands-on development of essential skills, we have the opportunity to guide and shape men on their journey of faith. As leaders, let us always strive to provide men with the tools they need to grow in their walk with God, encouraging them to embrace vulnerability, take ownership of their issues, seek reconciliation, and exercise wisdom. Additionally, let us equip them with the spiritual, decision-making, leadership, and mentoring skills necessary to navigate life as devoted followers of Christ. By embracing the KMS mindset, we can truly make a lasting impact on the lives of those we mentor and lead, helping them become the best versions of themselves.

GOD'S WORD IS ESSENTIAL FOR A MAN'S GROWTH: IT'S THE GUIDE

As men on a journey toward spiritual maturity, especially those of us called to lead in Bible study, immersing ourselves in Scripture is not just helpful; it's essential. The Bible stands as more than a mere historical record. It embodies the living, breathing Words of God, words that possess the power to transform lives and mold character. When we engage in the sacred scripture, we're not just reading, we're engaging with the spiritual force that shapes and defines our being as men.

First | God's Word Awakens Spiritual Discernment

> *"The natural person does not accept the things of the Spirit of God, for they are folly to him, and he is not able to understand them because they are spiritually discerned." — 1 Corinthians 2:14*

While human wisdom might help a man navigate the complexities of life, true discernment - the kind that aligns with the divine - is awakened through God's Word. It's like being handed a new set of eyes, ones that see beyond the surface and discern the spiritual realities that weave through our existence.

Second | God's Word Illuminates & Untwists the Mind

"There are some things in them that are hard to understand, which the ignorant and unstable twist to their own destruction, as they do the other Scriptures." — 2 Peter 3:16

"When the Spirit of truth comes, he will guide you into all the truth..." — John 16:13

Our minds, often clouded with misconceptions and twisted beliefs, need the clarifying light of scripture. Just as a lamp dispels darkness, God's Word penetrates our minds, exposing and untwisting the false beliefs that lead us astray. In its light, we find clarity and truth.

Third | God's Word Directs Men to Humility

"He leads the humble in what is right, and teaches the humble his way." — Psalm 25:8-9

"In humility count others more significant than yourselves." — Philippians 2:3-5

God's Word has a unique way of ushering men into a posture of humility. It's a journey from pride to humility, from self-sufficiency to reliance on God. This transformation is crucial for true spiritual growth and is something that human efforts alone cannot achieve.

Fourth | God's Word Works Truth into the Conscience

"We refuse to practice cunning or to tamper with God's word, but by the open statement of the truth we would commend ourselves to everyone's conscience in the sight of God." — 2 Corinthians 4:2

The Word of God does a deeper work than mere behavior modification; it embeds truth in our conscience. This is where integrity is born and nurtured, in the hidden places of the heart, guided by the unwavering truth of scripture.

Fifth | God's Word Aligns Us With The Most Unyielding & Unstoppable Will in the Universe

"If anyone's will is to do God's will, he will know whether the teaching is from God..." — John 7:17

In aligning our wills with God's, we tap into a source of obedience and power unparalleled in the universe. It's a will that moves mountains, changes hearts, and accomplishes the impossible.

Sixth | God's Word Reveals Wonderful Things

"Open my eyes, that I may behold wondrous things out of your law." — Psalm 119:18

The Bible is a treasure trove of wonders, each verse a gateway to profound insights and revelations. To uncover these wonders, we need only to open our hearts and minds to God's Word.

In conclusion, the Bible is not just a book; it's the very essence of God's voice to us. As men, when we engage with it deeply and consistently, it becomes our guide, our mentor, and our path to spiritual growth. It does what no human wisdom can - it transforms us from the inside out, aligning us with God's will and purpose for our lives. Therefore, let us not merely read the Word; let us live it, breathe it, and let it shape our very being.

FIVE DISCIPLINES TO BUILD INTO EVERY MAN

The end goal of the Christian life is to become the man that God wants us to be. We do this by allowing his vision, mission, purposes, and goals to shape our lives. One way we can lead men to this is through discipline. A discipline, or in our case, "spiritual discipline," is a training activity that helps to shape and mold character over an extended period of time that accelerates and focuses the process. Spiritual discipline is the "strict training" that Paul was talking about 1 Corinthians 9:25.

> *"Everyone who competes in the games goes into strict training."*
> *— 1 Corinthians 9:25*

One | Prayer

Prayer is a fundamental discipline, and men need to learn to build prayer routines into the daily patterns of their lives. Prayer is merely talking with God. For newer Christians, talking to an unseen God is unusual. It seems unusual because when we are having a conversation, there is usually someone physically standing in front of us who talks back. Prayer does not exactly work like this. But the small hurdle of learning to talk with an unseen God is not the central issue men have with practicing the discipline of prayer. The primary problem is all the other pressing issues that keep us from praying and developing a pattern of prayer. Daily we face demands that compete for our time. Because of this, men go days, weeks, and even months devoid of prayer, trusting only in human effort rather than also trusting in God through prayer. This can leave men feeling physically exhausted and spiritually depleted. Since so many other things compete with this priority, we need to be reminded of its priority and encourage men to strive to make time.

Two | Scripture

People want the truth, and I believe they're on a search for it. As Christians, we believe truth originates from God alone. God's Word is the revelation of the truth, and Jesus is the physical representation of truth. But we cannot know the truth if we don't know how to spend time in the Word and with Jesus. And small doses of it, spoon-fed in short readings one time a week on a Sunday morning is not enough. Men must be challenged to read the Bible, but they also must be taught how to read it, study it, memorize it, and pray it. Please remember it's not enough to inspire a man on the importance of the Bible and challenge him to read it—he must be taught how to do it. We must teach men how to read and study the Bible; it's the greatest gift we will ever give a man. And it's the primary way we hear from God. The following are a few pointers on how to get started.

First, just start reading. I would recommend starting in the New Testament with the Gospel of John with a Bible app for your phone. Make sure and choose an easy-to-read version like the New International

Version (NIV). Two of the great apps over the last few years that I have pointed men to is the Daily Audio Bible and the YouVersion Bible app.

Second, read a trusted devotional. Short and easy-to-read devotionals teach us how to dig meaning from the Bible. I would use a devotional that includes Bible verses and then expands on these verses. When it comes from a trusted person or trusted source, it helps you to learn how to draw practical applications from your Bible reading. It's like having a personal coach as you focus on a few verses from the scripture. Try the Men's Daily Devotional; it does just this, and is focused exclusively on men and our issues.

Third, establish regular patterns. This step is not so much about quantity or quality—it's about developing a routine. Setting small daily goals and repeating them is essential. Even 5 minutes per day for a month will result in positive habits and will become rewarding over time. Then increase the repetitions and the length of time as needed.

Finally, go to the next level by learning how to study the Bible. This is a little more involved and requires more effort, but it's the greatest gift you could ever give yourself or another man. I would use the Inductive Bible Study Method - Observe, Interpret, and Apply (as mentioned earlier). This method teaches men how to observe, interpret, and apply God's Word correctly. While it's great to learn from a pastor and discover how they observe, interpret, and apply the Bible, every man should learn how to discover the truths in God's Word for themselves.

Three | Brotherhood

Men need relationships with other men. Most men not only fail to develop meaningful relationships with other men, but they also lack adding in the spiritual component that must undergird it. Men prefer to go life alone for several reasons—time is valuable, relationships take work, chemistry is challenging, and autonomy is easier. But the biggest reason I believe men don't establish spiritual connections with other men is that they have never experienced one before. Having never had one, they don't know how to do it, and because of this, they have never experienced the benefit. All this leads to men defaulting to superficial male relationships that focus on trivial matters. They press the easy button.

Men who participate in one-on-one relationships or small groups mature faster than those who do not. This environment is a place where the previous three disciplines can be sharpened and experienced. Men need to be involved in a Christian community and not just the occasional weekend gathering. Smaller gatherings regularly are where men can discover some things about themselves and others. Spiritual growth doesn't happen in isolation; it occurs in a community, and men need other men. When men link arms, great things happen. Take, for example, Jesus and his men. What Jesus did changed the world, but without other men, the world would have never heard the good news Jesus proclaimed.

Four | Accountability

Accountability with another man is perhaps the leading indicator of spiritual success in a man's life. Brothers in accountable relationships make a great man of God. Jonathan made David better. Barnabas made Paul better. Paul made Timothy better. Jesus made the Twelve better. And it wasn't just happenstance and acquaintance; it was intentional brotherhood with substantial doses of accountability.

Spiritual accountability is perhaps one of the most misunderstood practices in male spiritual relationships. I believe this is because when men hear the word "accountability" in a religious context, they immediately assume a negative connotation. Men mostly hear about a need for accountability when issues of sin arise. Therefore, accountability means that we need help because we can't overcome our financial problems, sexual addictions, or marital conflicts. This understanding is unfortunate because it has given accountability a bad name and leaves out all the spiritual potential of accountability in brotherhood. If we brand accountability this way, it makes a man look weak, and men don't want to feel and look this way—unless they are in desperate need of help and don't care.

Here are a few things we need to understand about accountability. First, it needs to be proactive and positive, not exclusively reactive and negative. Spiritual accountability should be focused on the things I should start doing and continue doing. While occasionally, we all need a little accountability around some areas of sin that I need to stop doing, failure to fill the void activities we've stopped with activities we need to start fails to initiate positive momentum. We need some accountability around actions that will have a proactive and positive impact on our spiritual life. For example, men need accountability in praying with their wives, regularly giving, reading Scripture, forgiving themselves, casting anxiety on God, and things like that. Second, men need to invite self-imposed accountability. Too often, we think someone else needs to hold us accountable, and I think this idea, while well-meaning, fails to work successfully. However, when a man invites self-imposed accountability based on declared goals, there is a much higher return and long-term benefit. Accountability of any kind that is self-imposed produces more significant results—this is especially true in this case. Third, accountability needs to be spiritually focused. We need men not only to hold us accountable but to help us dig for the spiritual aspects. Accountability to behavior change is essential but add in the spiritual purpose and potential spiritual outcomes of it, and then we focus on doing the right behaviors for the right reasons. We have to remember we are becoming the men God wants us to be, and we are doing it for his glory, not our own. Therefore, when it comes to accountability, here is what we are looking for: positive, willing spiritual accountability.

Five | Personal Ministry

Christian men who are accelerating their spiritual growth are involved in personal ministry. Personal ministry includes things like leading a small group, mentoring other men, teaching a class, organizing a mission trip experience, serving on the board of a non-profit, or conducting a study in a workplace environment. I get excited when men do this because now they are moving from being disciples to discipling others. They are finding unique ways to use their gifts, passions, and talents for kingdom benefits.

Some men need to be pushed to take this step. Too often, men wait too long before taking this step. I think men sometimes need a little push on this one since they prefer to disqualify themselves for lack of knowledge and because of personal sin. They need another man to say, "Get off the bench and into the game."

BUILDING & SUSTAINING A QUIET TIME WITH GOD

Our lives are filled with appointments and meetings, but there is one appointment that we find hard to keep consistent. Missing this one appointment produces guilt and failure in many men: it's having a daily quiet time with God. But this regular appointment with God doesn't have to be so daunting and should be a source of life, joy, truth, direction, and a means of deepening our relationship with the God who loves us.

One | Company with Jesus is imperative.

It's hard to comprehend, but God created us for a relationship with him, and he loves us when we choose to spend time with him. Often, I picture God sitting in an empty chair across from me when I take time to be with him. After all, he's there with me. I imagine myself talking to a close friend—who happens to be the Creator of the universe. Men like Moses, Abraham, David, Joshua, and even Jesus implied that they communicated to God in much of the same way. They often prayed out loud just like they would any other conversation. These conversations were ways they invested in what was a primary and essential relationship for them.

We wouldn't dream of neglecting a close friend. We spend time with these friends because they give us life, connection, wisdom, and support. We need their company in regular doses. And it's no different with God. Except he's not just any man, friend, or relationship, he's the ultimate source of life.

Jesus put it this way. "I am the vine; you are the branches. If a man remains in me and I in him, he will bear much fruit; apart from me, you can do nothing . . . If you remain in me and my words remain in you, ask whatever you wish, and it will be given you. This is to my Father's glory, that you bear much fruit, showing yourself to be my disciples." (John 15:5-8). Did you notice the operative word in Jesus' instruction? It's remaining: remaining in him. Having a daily quiet time with God is a vital method for "remaining in him and he in us."

Two | Don't overcomplicate a quiet time with God.

What kinds of things do you do with a close friend? You invest time with them. At times, it's as simple as a quick phone call to hear what's going on with them and share what's going on with you. It is no different when we meet with God. We take some time alone with God, maybe 6 -12 minutes at the start of each day. During this time, listen to him by reading a text from God's word and talk to him in conversational prayer. Sometimes you might like to prepare yourself with a song of worship at the start as a way of praising him.

Think of your meeting with God as an alignment meeting to get each day started right. In quietness, bring your needs to him, confess your sin, ask for his help, learn from him through meditation on the text, and worship him as our Lord. Time with him daily will incrementally change your heart and mind, and as a result, you will become more like him.

Three | Remember to keep it regular.

Our relationship with God is only as new as the last time we were with him. So keep it regular with a daily appointment. Sometimes it may be just touching base for a few minutes. And other times we may have more extended time with him, but don't neglect the best, the most forgiving, loving, and gracious friend you will ever have: God.

A possible pattern for a quiet time with God.

[2-3 Minutes] Preparing for the meeting.

Start to slow by preparing for your quiet time with a period of silence, praise, or reflection. The goal in preparation is to move from thinking about the cares of the world to thinking about your relationship with God. During this time, you will want to note where you are personally and the current state of your heart, mind, and soul. It may be good to write out critical concerns in a journal or notepad so that you can move from "your self-concerns" to a posture of engaging God.

[2-3 Minutes] Listen to God by reading a relevant scripture.

Next, take a couple of minutes to find verses that speak to the concerns you noted. I love the Open Bible's Topic search tool for this: www.openbible.info/topics. Just type in a word or phrase, and you will find a ton of relevant verses. Stop at the one that speaks to you and listen to God's word to you. During this time, just let God speak. Read the verse multiple times, looking at God's instruction for your situation.

It might be good to write out the actions or steps God's word suggests you take.

[2-3 Minutes] Talk to God by sharing your needs.

Finally, talk to God about your situation, the direction scripture is leading you, and the challenges you are facing. The A.C.T.S. method is a great model for this conversation time. It begins with Adoration: revering God for what he has done. Next, Confess: this is to own the sin that God has brought to your mind during your reading. Next, Thanksgiving: appreciate God for what he has done or revealed to you. Finally, Supplication: ask God for what you might need for the day.

In 6-12 daily minutes, you will not only be centered for a new day, but you will deepen your relationship with the God of the universe who wants to be in a loving relationship with you. Try this pattern for 30 days and your relationship with God will be more profound and the outcomes unbelievable.

BUILDING A BIBLE-READING HABIT

When it comes to helping men read the Bible, most feel like they are stepping into unknown territory. It's a common hurdle, especially for those of us leading others who are just beginning their faith journey. Here's a simple, practical guide you can share to help them get started:

One | Start with the Gospel of John

Encourage them to begin with the Gospel of John. This book is an excellent starting point for anyone new to the Bible. It's an eyewitness account from John, a disciple of Jesus, covering the life, teachings, death, and resurrection of Christ. It's the essence of the Christian faith, written in a way that's engaging and insightful.

Two | Suggest Reading One Chapter a Day

Urge them to take it slow and steady - one chapter a day. The Bible is rich and deep, and it's not about how quickly one can read through it, but how much they can absorb and apply. Reading one chapter a day helps in building a sustainable habit, allowing them to reflect deeply on the teachings of each chapter.

Three | Focus on a Keyword or Phrase

Guide them to look for a keyword or phrase in each chapter that speaks to them. Here's what they can do with it:

- **Underline It:** Suggest that they underline or note down the words or phrases that stand out. This helps in personalizing their reading experience.
- **Pray It:** Encourage them to bring these words into their prayers. This can be a way to seek deeper understanding and guidance.
- **Share It:** Motivate them to keep these words in mind throughout their day and share them if they feel led. This can be a great way to witness and encourage others.

Fostering a Lifelong Habit

Remind them that this journey with the Bible is about forming a lasting connection with God's Word. It's about creating a routine that nurtures their spiritual growth and understanding. As they walk through the Gospel of John, each chapter can become a step towards a deeper faith and a stronger relationship with God.

Brothers, as we guide our fellow men in this journey, let's remind them (and ourselves) that the Bible is a living, breathing guide for life. It's not just about reading a book; it's about encountering God and letting His Word transform us from the inside out. Let's walk this path together, building each other up in faith and wisdom.

GET GODLY ADVICE AS A MAN AND LEADER

Who do you turn to for advice? Maybe it's your spouse, pastor, or a trusted friend. If you're consulting these people, you're on the right track. But remember, seeking good advice is more than a simple task. Every decision, big or small, can send ripples through your life. I'm not saying you should delay decisions out of fear. But I am emphasizing the importance of grounding your choices in a process that aligns with God's will, which includes seeking Godly advice—with a capital "G."

Take note of this crucial point: Godly advice is just one part of discerning God's will. It's a complex process, and many have written extensively about it. You're on solid ground when your decision 1) aligns with God's Word, 2) feels prompted by the Holy Spirit, and 3) fits your circumstances. But not all choices are clear-cut. That's where Godly counsel, combined with other key indicators, comes in. Proverbs underscores its significance:

> "Where there is no guidance, a people falls, but in an abundance of counselors there is safety." — Proverbs 11:14

"Whoever walks with the wise becomes wise, but the companion of fools will suffer harm." — *Proverbs 13:20*

"Without counsel plans fail, but with many advisers they succeed." — *Proverbs 15:22*

So, whom should you consult? Remember King Rehoboam's mistake in 1 Kings 12. He ignored the seasoned advisors who knew his father, King Solomon, and instead listened to his peers, leading to a divided kingdom. The lesson? Choose your advisors wisely:

Seek out those with life experience and spiritual insight who consistently turn to God for direction.

Consult not just those with experience but also those who've faced similar decisions. What did they learn?

Avoid the trap of only seeking agreement. The popular or easy choice isn't always the right one.

Proverbs 3:5-6 advises, "Trust in the Lord with all your heart, and do not lean on your own understanding. In all your ways acknowledge Him, and He will make straight your paths." Real men acknowledge their limits. In Decision Making & the Will of God, Garry Friesen highlights the right attitude for wisdom: humility, teachability, reverence, diligence, uprightness, and faith. His decision-making framework includes:

- Praying for wisdom;
- Diving into Scripture;
- Conducting personal research;
- Seeking wise counsel; and
- Reflecting on your experiences.

Ultimately, the best source of counsel is God. And let's be real–even with our best efforts, we'll sometimes falter. But God is ever-present, capable of turning our missteps into good and guiding us back on track. So let's march forward, confident that as we grow spiritually, our decision-making will also improve, partly because we've chosen our advisors well.

THE IMPORTANCE OF ACCOUNTABILITY FOR MEN

Embarking on a spiritual journey often conjures images of solitary contemplation and personal struggle. However, this perception overlooks a key aspect of Christian growth: the power of relationships and accountability. In a culture that frequently glorifies the rugged, self-reliant individual, epitomized by figures like Jason Bourne, the biblical call to communal living and mutual support presents a strikingly different narrative. For Christian men, both as leaders, and as followers, understanding and embracing accountability is paramount. It's not only beneficial for personal faith development but also crucial in guiding and strengthening those we lead. As men committed to deepening our faith and embodying our convictions, incorporating accountability into our spiritual lives becomes a dual responsibility. Here we will explore five transformative ways to integrate accountability into the fabric of our spiritual journey. This approach ensures that our path is not only personally enriching but also profoundly grounded in the supportive fellowship that God desires for us and for the men we lead.

One | Stop Avoiding Relationships

Often, men are intensely private about their inner worlds. This guardedness can stem from pride, a barrier that prevents us from acknowledging our deeper needs or sharing them, as it reveals our vulnerabilities. In the realm of spiritual accountability, pride frequently hinders progress. Humility acknowledges the need for relationships, while pride resists the vulnerability they require. This connects directly to the next point.

Two | Invite Honest Feedback

As men striving for humility, we must be open to feedback. This involves first recognizing our need for help and then inviting trusted, Christ-following men into our lives for support. Genuine feedback is possible only within authentic, trusting relationships.

Three | Request Specific Accountability

Every Christian needs accountability tailored to their unique struggles and vulnerabilities. Without genuine connections, we cannot grow into better men. Accountability must be specific and measurable; otherwise, we won't see tangible results. It involves a choice: avoid detailed accountability and take the easy path or embrace it and choose the more challenging route. The latter, though it may involve discomfort or change, leads to positive growth.

Four | Foster Positive Accountability

Often, we resist accountability because it feels authoritarian. But accountability isn't just about adhering to rules or feeling inadequate. It can be a source of mutual encouragement in following Jesus. Remember, the New Testament frequently exhorts us to "encourage one another."

By reframing accountability as a positive experience, we can transform it into a source of mutual growth.

Five | Celebrate Small Victories

In our spiritual journey, we will never fully "arrive" until we meet Jesus. However, every small step towards Christ is significant. Philippians 3:16 says, "Only let us live up to what we have already attained." This implies living out what we know and continuously growing. By recognizing and celebrating these incremental steps, we acknowledge and reinforce our progress.

In conclusion, building accountability into our spiritual lives is not just a recommendation but a vital step towards authentic Christian living. By embracing relationships, inviting honest feedback, seeking specific accountability, reframing it positively, and celebrating small victories, we align ourselves more closely with God's design for communal growth and personal development. These steps, though challenging, pave the way for a more fulfilling and impactful faith journey. As we walk this path together, let us remember that in our shared struggles and triumphs, we find not only personal growth but also the profound strength and beauty of our shared journey in Christ.

6 PRESCRIPTIONS FOR THE GODLY MAN

In the realm of personal growth, especially spiritual growth, we often encounter two distinct approaches: prescription and description. A description tells us what is, painting a picture of the current state or characteristics of a person or situation. Prescription, on the other hand, is more proactive and directional – it's a strong sanction on what needs to be done.

For a godly man seeking to grow in his faith and life, understanding this difference is crucial. Descriptions help us understand where we are, but prescriptions show us the path to where we need to be. Let's dig into six vital prescriptions that can transform the life of a man who desires to walk closely with God.

Prescription One: Priority for God

The foremost prescription for a godly man is to give God the highest priority in his life. This means consciously placing God at the center of all decisions, actions, and thoughts. It's not just about attending church on Sundays or reading the Bible occasionally; it's about living in a way that every aspect of life is influenced and guided by a relationship with

God. This could manifest in daily devotions, prayer, and consistently seeking God's wisdom in every situation.

Prescription Two: Receptivity

Receptivity here refers to the openness to God's word, His teachings, and His correction. It's about being moldable and teachable in the hands of God. A receptive heart is essential for growth and transformation. It involves listening for God's voice in every circumstance and being willing to change direction or mindset when prompted by the Holy Spirit.

Prescription Three: Identity Formation

For a godly man, identity is not formed by worldly standards or personal achievements but is rooted in Christ. This prescription is about understanding and embracing who we are in God's eyes. It involves recognizing our value and purpose as defined by God, not by our careers, accomplishments, or societal status. This secure identity in Christ leads to confidence and peace, unaffected by life's fluctuating circumstances.

Prescription Four: Spiritual Discipline

Spiritual discipline encompasses practices like prayer, fasting, Bible study, and worship. These are not just religious activities but means to deepen our relationship with God. They are tools that help in cultivating a spiritually disciplined life, where one is consistently growing in faith and understanding of God's word. This discipline helps in building resilience and strength to face life's challenges.

Prescription Five: Integrated Character

An integrated character is one that is consistent in all areas of life – private, public, professional, and spiritual. This means living out godly principles not just in comfortable or religious settings but in every aspect of life. It's about integrity, honesty, and demonstrating Christ-like behavior in all interactions and decisions.

Prescription Six: Pure Motivation

Lastly, the motivation behind our actions should stem from a pure heart. This involves doing things not for personal gain, recognition, or approval from others but out of a sincere desire to serve God and others. It's about aligning our motives with God's will, ensuring that our actions reflect our faith and commitment to Him.

In summary, these six prescriptions: Priority for God, Receptivity, Identity Formation, Spiritual Discipline, Integrated Character, and Pure Motivation are not just guidelines but life-transforming principles that, when applied, lead to a deeper, more meaningful relationship with God. They challenge us to grow and mature in our faith, becoming men who not only understand their God-given purpose but live it out in every aspect of their lives.

HELPING MEN BATTLE HURTS, HABITS, & HANG-UPS

In our relentless battle against sin it's crucial to remember that our journey is not just about our individual struggles but also about guiding and supporting our fellow men in their own battles. Jesus Christ's victory over sin on the cross, while complete and all-encompassing, is not a license for us to continue sinning. Instead, it's an invitation to a higher life, one that emulates His sinless nature. This reality dismantles the common, yet flawed, excuses of human imperfection and highlights the true potential of our humanity.

Our fight against sin is deeply rooted in our love for Jesus and our commitment to being credible witnesses of His transformative love. It's about growing into the fullness of the men God created us to be and drawing nearer to Him through His grace and mercy.

This battle, however, is internal and demands wisdom and a well-thought-out strategy. As men guiding other men, we need to identify and tackle three main categories of sin: hurts, habits, and hang-ups.

One | Hurts

We've all been wounded, sometimes by those closest to us. These injuries can foster a tendency to cling to unforgiveness. Yet, Jesus teaches us to forgive as we have been forgiven. In guiding other men, we emphasize the liberation found in releasing unforgiveness and embracing Christ's example of forgiveness, love, grace, and mercy.

Two | Habits

We all struggle with repetitive behaviors that can be harmful. Common issues include greed, selfishness, overconsumption, and harmful language. As leaders and mentors, we must model and encourage the abandonment of these harmful habits, replacing them with life-giving practices that reflect Jesus' character and light to the world.

Three | Hang-ups

Every man faces personal roadblocks, whether deep-seated family patterns or personal insecurities. As guides, we share our own experiences of overcoming these challenges through the strength and guidance of the Holy Spirit. We encourage our brothers in Christ to lean on God's strength to navigate and overcome these hurdles.

In this journey, we remind our brothers that we are not alone. The Father, Son, and Holy Spirit support us, and as a community of believers, we support each other. Our pride must not deceive us into thinking we can win this battle alone. It's a daily, ongoing fight, and while we may stumble, we must always turn back to Jesus Christ. In submitting to Him, we share in His ultimate victory.

We echo Paul's words in Ephesians 6:10-11, urging our fellow men to be strong in the Lord and to equip themselves with the full armor of God. This spiritual armor is vital not only for our personal battles:

it helps us stand alongside our brothers, empowering and supporting them in their struggles against sin. In Christ, we find not just individual victory, but collective triumph as a community of men dedicated to living out His truth.

FOR GOD'S SAKE, LET YOUR MEN PRAY

For men to truly embrace their faith and grow in their relationship with God, it's crucial that they not just learn about prayer but actively engage in it. Experiencing prayer firsthand is the key to understanding its profound impact. Why do we pray? Consider the prayers you've known since childhood, like "Now I lay me down to sleep," or "God is great, God is good," and of course, the Lord's Prayer. These prayers incorporate requests and thanksgiving, and Jesus, in the Lord's Prayer, gives us a framework for prayer. But the essence of prayer extends beyond these elements.

Let's explore why it's vital for men to not just know about prayer, but to immerse themselves in it:

First | Engaging in Divine Dialogue

Prayer isn't merely a one-way conversation; it's an intimate dialogue with God. He exists as a personal being – Father, Son, and Holy Spirit. When men engage in prayer, they connect directly with the Divine. It's crucial to understand that while we often do the talking, pausing and embracing silence allows us to hear God's part of the conversation.

Second | Cultivating Intimacy with God

True intimacy with God goes beyond reciting needs or facts. It involves opening up with honesty and vulnerability, sharing our deepest needs, desires, and emotions with Him. This open communication builds a closer relationship with our Heavenly Father.

Third | Experiencing Transformational Power

Each prayerful encounter with God initiates a change within us. This transformation brings us closer to realizing our God-given potential. It's important to remember that God remains unchanging – it is we who are transformed by prayer. This change can manifest as a sudden conviction, a miraculous shift, or a gradual progression, but it always leads to a profound inner transformation.

Therefore, prayer is much more than a ritual; it's a bridge to the divine, a channel through which we experience God's presence. Regular prayer sharpens our ability to discern His voice and comprehend His will. By actively engaging in prayer, men open themselves up to these transformative experiences. As noted by theologian John Stott, prayer is not about bending God's will to ours but aligning our will to His.

Encouraging men to pray allows them to explore a deeper connection with God, fostering growth, vulnerability, and transformation. It's through these moments of prayerful surrender that men discover their true strength and purpose.

SHOULDER TO SHOULDER: THE MISSING LINK FOR MEN

It's time to confront a hard truth: men desperately need each other. Yet our culture often sells us a different story. It glorifies the lone wolf, the self-made man, the independent hero who doesn't need anyone. We're bombarded with messages saying, "Real men stand alone." This narrative has been so ingrained in us that, startlingly, most men today lack a close male friend. Can we really say this is healthy or beneficial?

The answer is a resounding no. The world's version of manhood is a far cry from the reality.

In truth, genuine strength is found in acknowledging our need for brotherhood. Autonomy might be our default mode, but authentic manhood flourishes in the context of community, particularly within the Christian brotherhood. Here we not only witness but also partake in the profound spiritual connection exemplified by the Trinity: Father, Son, and Holy Spirit. It's in this sacred fellowship that our faith takes on flesh and blood, radiating love, unity, and God's transformative message of grace and reconciliation. Brotherhood is where we truly sharpen each other, creating a space that guards against life's disasters that threaten to unravel the very fabric of our manhood.

But how do we foster this life-giving brotherhood? How do we embrace the "iron sharpens iron" dynamic that is so vital? Here are three actionable steps:

One | Transparency

It's time to drop the masks. Facing our challenges head-on requires honesty about our struggles. Rooted in our identity in Christ and the freedom His sacrifice grants us, we must move past the fears and shame that lead us to hide. Let's commit to authenticity, embracing vulnerability as we break free from sin's shackles.

Two | Accountability

Embrace accountability with our brothers, not merely as a deterrent from wrong but as a catalyst for right. This accountability should be twofold-a firm hand to hold us back from missteps and a supportive push toward our God-given potential. It's about saying, "I stand with you; let's pursue God's call together."

Three | Consistency

Intentionality is key. Brotherhood doesn't happen by chance; it's a deliberate choice. Set regular times to connect, whether it's bi-monthly or more frequent. Let's deepen these connections beyond the superficial, fostering relationships that challenge and encourage us in our spiritual journey. Remember the exhortation in Hebrews 10:24-25 about spurring each other towards love and good works, not neglecting our meetings but encouraging each other.

Jesus was the ultimate nonconformist. He never yielded to misguided societal norms. His life and teachings underscore the indispensability of Christian brotherhood for our spiritual vitality. This isn't an optional extra; it's essential. As Paul urges us in Romans 12:10, "Love one another with brotherly affection. Outdo one another in showing honor." Brothers, let's embrace this radical call. Let's commit to forging deep, godly bonds that defy cultural expectations and lead us closer to Christ. Together, let's redefine manhood.

SECTION 3

PRACTICAL TOOLS FOR MINISTRY TO MEN

FAT —
men

FAITHFUL

AVAILABLE

TEACHABLE

— THEY ARE HUNGRY —

RECRUITING MEN: THE 3 M'S

When embarking on the journey of building men, you will be laying the foundation for a thriving men's ministry. This checklist is your roadmap to not only transform individual lives but also to establish a strong community of men dedicated to growing in faith together.

One | Identify the Men

Your mission begins with identifying the men who will form the core of your men's ministry. I am always doing two things here: First, I am selecting men, and I don't wait for them to show up. Putting announcements in the bulletin does not work. Do it like Jesus. Go out and get the ones you want. Second, when I am looking for men I am looking for spiritually "hungry" men. They are always the H.O.T. men (see the chapter entitled H.O.T. Men Make Stronger Connections). Then invite them along. Men love to be invited and challenged. Do you have a list? If not, make a list now:

1) FAT - FAITHFUL, AVAILABLE, TEACHABLE
2) Identify MATERIAL
3) Identify - Time/Location

4)

5)

Two | Identify the Materials

Selecting your materials will, by nature, choose the direction and building blocks for your men's ministry. Different resources can significantly impact the dynamics within your group. Be intentional in your selection, ensuring that the materials align with the goals of both individual growth and the broader ministry.

Here is a layout of some materials and how they might support or hinder what you are trying to build:

THE CARE & SUPPORT GROUP

- Goal: Stability & Recovery
- Impact: Restoration & Care
- Examples: Financial Peace University, Divorce Care, and Celebrate Recovery
- Leadership Type: Counselor

THE STUDY GROUP

- Goal: Knowledge
- Impact: Understanding
- Examples: Bible Study Fellowship and Community Bible Study
- Leadership Type: Teacher

THE LIFE GROUP

- Goal: Community
- Impact: Relationship & Friendship
- Examples: Topical Books, Social Activity, and Sermon Series Focused
- Leadership Type: Connector

THE DISCIPLESHIP GROUP

- Goal: Missional Living
- Impact: Behavior, Motives & Multiplication
- Examples: Resolute, Navigators, and Cru
- Leadership Type: Facilitator

Three | Identify the Meeting Time and Location

While you can't accommodate every schedule and preference, you can accommodate yourself. This should take place at a time and location that works best for you so that you can invite others, too. This is vital in the early stages of building your ministry because you need to be present to give it direction.

- When will you meet?
- Where will you meet?

In summary, this checklist serves as the blueprint for building men and a men's ministry that will impact lives and communities. Your devotionals, books, and unique voice will be instrumental in guiding men towards a deeper faith journey within the context of a growing and thriving men's ministry.

MINISTRY: STARTING A MEN'S MINISTRY IN A SMALL CHURCH

In the heart of every small church lies a potent opportunity: the chance to forge a men's ministry that, while perhaps limited in size, is immeasurable in impact. The beauty of a smaller congregation is the intimacy and strength of its connections, making each step towards fostering a men's ministry not just achievable but deeply meaningful. At the same time, this also sometimes prevents it.

The following are several practical steps to cultivating a vibrant men's ministry within the cozy confines of a small church. By focusing on the strengths of the small church environment, like mentorship, fellowship, service, and the like, we can create an environment where men not only grow in their faith but also in their bonds with one another. Let's explore how even the smallest congregations can make a significant impact on the lives of their men.

Here are nine gradual building blocks to consider:

One | Be A Godly Man Worthy Of Following: In a small church, personal conduct is even more visible. Model the Christian virtues in your daily life. This can have a ripple effect, encouraging others to follow suit.

Two | Initiate Informal Mentorship: Formal mentorship programs might be unnecessary with fewer men. Instead, focus on building one-on-one relationships. Share life lessons, discuss faith, and offer guidance in an informal setting.

Three | Create One Small Group: Even with a few men, start a small group dedicated to discussing faith, life challenges, and scripture. This can be a weekly or bi-weekly gathering where men feel safe to share and grow together.

Four | Engage In Service: Organize small, manageable service projects that the men can undertake together. It could be helping a needy family in the church or community or a simple church maintenance project. This builds camaraderie and a sense of accomplishment.

Five | Foster Conversations: In smaller settings, it's easier to encourage open communication. Create an environment where men feel comfortable sharing without judgment, whether it's during coffee after service or in a more structured group setting.

Six | Utilize Digital Resources: If organizing events or retreats is challenging, consider virtual resources like webinars, online conferences, or digital men's groups. This can provide access to broader content and community without needing large-scale organization.

Seven | Start A Prayer Chain or Group Text: Start a simple prayer chain where men can request and offer prayers for each other. This can be done via group emails, texts, or a dedicated time during services.

Eight | Encourage Daily Devotionals: Suggest or provide resources for daily devotionals. This can be a powerful tool for individual spiritual growth and can be discussed in group settings for collective learning.

Nine | Celebrate Personal Growth and Milestones: In a smaller community, personal achievements in faith can be recognized and celebrated more intimately. Acknowledge these milestones to encourage continued growth and participation.

Implementing these in a small church can create a strong foundation for a thriving men's ministry, fostering spiritual growth and a supportive community among the men.

MINISTRY: STARTING A MEN'S MINISTRY IN A MID-SIZED CHURCH

Embarking on the journey to establish a men's ministry in a mid-sized church, especially where a robust and large women's ministry already thrives, is an endeavor that calls for a careful, strategic, and intentional approach. This venture is not just about creating another church group; it's about fostering a space where men can explore, grow, and strengthen their faith alongside their fellow brothers in Christ. In a world where the needs and roles of men are ever-evolving, this guide aims to provide you with a foundational blueprint to initiate a men's ministry that resonates with the hearts and minds of the men in your congregation. It's about building a ministry that complements the existing women's ministry, thereby enriching the entire church community with a balanced and holistic approach to spiritual growth and fellowship.

Here's a step-by-step guide to get started:

One | Assess the Need and Interest: Begin by gauging the interests and needs of the men in your church. This can be done through informal conversations, surveys, or a meeting specifically called for this purpose. Understanding what the men in your church are looking for in a ministry is crucial.

Two | Learn from the Women's Ministry: If there is an existing women's ministry, take time to understand what makes the women's ministry successful. Is it their structure, types of events, or leadership style? Learning from their strengths can provide valuable insights for starting the men's ministry.

Three | Seek the Support of Leadership: Discuss your vision with the church leadership. Explain how a men's ministry could complement and balance the existing women's ministry, contributing to the overall health of the church.

Four | Form a Small Leadership Team: Identify a few committed men who share your vision and are willing to take on leadership roles. This team will be instrumental in planning, organizing, and leading the ministry.

Five | Define the Vision and Goals: Clearly articulate the vision and goals of the men's ministry. What are its core values? What does it aim to achieve? How will it serve the men in the church and the community?

Six | Start with Small, Targeted Initiatives: Instead of launching with a big event, start with small, focused activities that meet the expressed needs and interests of the men. This could be a Bible study group, a service project, or a series of workshops on topics relevant to men.

Seven | Promote and Communicate Effectively: Use church marketing points, bulletin, announcements, social media, and word-of-mouth to promote the men's ministry. Clear communication about the purpose, events, and how to get involved is key.

Eight | Collaborate with the Women's Ministry: Seek opportunities for joint events or projects with the women's ministry. This fosters church unity and allows both ministries to learn from each other and share resources.

Nine | Regularly Evaluate and Adapt: Continuously assess the effectiveness of the men's ministry. Seek feedback from participants and be willing to adjust to better meet the needs of the men.

Ten | Cultivate an Invitational Environment: Ensure that the ministry is welcoming to all men, regardless of their age, background, or stage in their faith journey. An inclusive approach will help in building a diverse and vibrant community.

Eleven | Pray and Seek God's Guidance: Throughout the process, continually seek God's guidance through prayer. A ministry grounded in prayer is more likely to align with God's will and have a lasting impact.

In conclusion, the journey to establish a vibrant and impactful men's ministry in your church is a path filled with both challenges and immense rewards. By thoughtfully assessing the needs of the men in your congregation, drawing insights from the successful women's ministry, garnering support from church leadership, and creating a small yet dedicated leadership team, you set the groundwork for a ministry that resonates deeply with its members. Remember, the key is to start with small, targeted initiatives that directly address the interests and needs of your men. Promote effective communication, collaborate with other ministries, continuously evaluate your progress, and above all, create an inviting environment that welcomes all. As you move forward, let prayer be the compass that guides your decisions and actions, aligning your ministry with God's will. With these steps, you are well on your way to nurturing a men's ministry that not only complements the women's ministry but stands as a testament to the power of faith, fellowship, and collective growth in Christ within your church community.

MINISTRY: PAY ATTENTION TO A MAN'S PAIN

Understanding the spiritual pain points of the common man is crucial for effective ministry and support. Men often grapple with unique challenges and struggles that can hinder their spiritual growth. By recognizing and addressing these issues, we can offer more meaningful support and guidance.

Here is a short list of areas where men experience pain today.

First | Identity and Purpose: Many men struggle with understanding their true identity and purpose in life. This can lead to feelings of inadequacy, confusion, and a lack of direction. In a world that often measures success by material achievements or social status, men may feel lost when they fail to meet these standards. The key here is to help men discover their identity in Christ and understand that their worth is not defined by worldly achievements but by their relationship with God.

Second | Isolation and Loneliness: Despite living in a digitally connected world, many men experience a deep sense of isolation and loneliness. Society's expectations of masculinity often discourage men from expressing vulnerability or seeking help. This can lead to a lack of deep, meaningful relationships and a sense of disconnection from others, including their families, friends, and faith communities. Encouraging men to form authentic relationships and be open about their struggles can be transformative.

Third | Responsibility and Leadership: Men often feel immense pressure to be providers, protectors, and leaders in their families and communities. This responsibility can become a burden, especially when they feel ill-equipped or when circumstances are challenging. Guiding men to understand and embrace their roles from a biblical perspective, highlighting the importance of servant leadership and reliance on God's wisdom, can alleviate this pressure.

Fourth | Temptation and Moral Struggles: Men are frequently confronted with various temptations and moral challenges, ranging from issues like lust and greed to anger and pride. These struggles can lead to feelings of guilt, shame, and spiritual stagnation. Providing a safe space for men to confess, seek accountability, and receive grace-filled guidance is vital.

Fifth | Faith and Doubt: Many men wrestle with questions about their faith, experiencing periods of doubt and uncertainty. These doubts can be about God's existence, His goodness, or His plan for their lives. Addressing these doubts openly and exploring them through scripture and community can strengthen their faith.

In dealing with the spiritual pain points that men face today, there are two practical pillars that serve as essential tools for healing and growth.

Bible (and its role in healing pain):
- **The Bible is an Anchor for Identity and Purpose:** The Bible offers a foundational understanding of identity and purpose. When men struggle with feelings of inadequacy or confusion about their place in the world, the Bible provides clarity and reassurance. It teaches that one's true identity is found in Christ (Galatians 2:20) and that our purpose extends beyond worldly achievements to fulfilling God's unique plan for each life (Jeremiah 29:11). This perspective helps men see beyond the transient measures of success and find a deeper sense of worth and direction.

- **The Bible is our Guidance through Moral Struggles and Temptations:** The Bible is a source of wisdom and strength in overcoming temptations and moral challenges. It offers not only guidelines for righteous living but also examples of individuals who struggled and overcame. Passages like 1 Corinthians 10:13 assure men that they are not alone in their struggles and that God provides a way to withstand temptation. This scriptural support is crucial for men dealing with guilt, shame, or spiritual stagnation.

Brotherhood of Faith (and its importance in addressing pain):
- **Brotherhood is the Antidote to Isolation and Loneliness:** Brotherhood creates a sense of community, breaking the cycle of isolation and loneliness many men experience. In a brotherhood, men find a

space where they can express vulnerability, share their struggles, and receive support. This kind of fellowship, encouraged in scriptures like Proverbs 27:17 ("As iron sharpens iron, so one person sharpens another"), helps men build deep, meaningful relationships that enrich their lives and faith.

- **Brotherhood is the Support in Navigating Responsibility and Leadership:** Brotherhood provides men with collective wisdom and support as they navigate their roles as providers, protectors, and leaders. In a community of peers, men can learn from each other's experiences and challenges. This support is invaluable in helping men understand and embrace their responsibilities from a biblical perspective, reducing the sense of burden and promoting a model of servant leadership.

In essence, the Bible and Brotherhood act as complementary pillars in addressing the spiritual pain points of men. The Bible provides divine guidance, wisdom, and reassurance, while brotherhood offers practical, real-world support and connection. Together, they form a robust framework for helping men navigate their spiritual journeys, overcome challenges, and grow in their faith.

But that's not all.

The Proactive Force of Bible & Brotherhood Help Us Avoid Pain

The dual pillars of the Bible and Brotherhood not only offer a reactive response to pain but also foster a proactive approach that can help men avoid many struggles. The Bible, with its timeless wisdom, equips men with principles and teachings that can preemptively guide decision-making and lifestyle choices, reducing the likelihood of encountering certain pains and struggles. It encourages a life lived in alignment with God's will, which inherently steers away from paths that lead to spiritual harm. Similarly, brotherhood acts as a proactive support system. In a community of like-minded individuals, men are not just reacting to challenges but are continuously sharpening each other, as described in Proverbs 27:17. This environment fosters accountability, mutual encouragement, and shared wisdom, which can prevent many of the pitfalls and isolation that lead to pain. Together, the Bible and brotherhood provide not just a sanctuary in times of trouble but also a roadmap and companionship for a journey that avoids many of the spiritual pitfalls men might otherwise face alone.

MINISTRY: QUALIFICATIONS FOR MEN'S LEADERS

Everyone has an opinion about what makes a good leader. Volumes and volumes of leadership books have been written on this subject. And yet, at the same time, it is easy to determine a great leader's qualities. All you need to do is look back on some of the great leaders you have known and followed and consider what qualities made them the best.

But within the church God has a prescribed plan, and the Apostle Paul lays it out. Mainly because Timothy needs him to get it right, considering the leadership mess in this church. In chapter three, Paul clarifies fourteen attributes that would qualify a man for spiritual leadership in the church. We are going to look at these qualifications in six categories, only because it is impossible in this limited space to discuss them all at length.

Before we get to this list, let's clarify what a qualification is. Qualifications are proficiencies that make someone suitable for an activity. For example, when you are looking for a job, there is usually a list of qualifying factors that an employer declares before you apply.

These qualifications are told to you beforehand, so, if necessary, you can qualify or disqualify yourself.

Let me pause here and address an issue a lot of men have when it comes to spiritual leadership. They have this tendency to disqualify themselves. I see this so often that I believe if disqualification were a qualification, every man would be very qualified. But instead of disqualifying yourself, I want you to hear each of these qualifications in an aspirational sense. I want you to reject the voice of disqualification and embrace the aspirational spirit of that quality and category. I want you to aspire to it because I think Paul has three intentions for this list: to disqualify some, qualify others, and inspire yet others.

So let's get to the list. Here are the 14 qualifications for leaders in the church, from 1 Timothy 3:1-7:

> *Therefore an overseer must be [1] above reproach, [2] the husband of one wife, [3] sober-minded, [4] self-controlled, [5] respectable, [6] hospitable, [7] able to teach, [8] not a drunkard, [9] not violent but gentle, [10] not quarrelsome, [11] not a lover of money. He must [12] manage his own household well, with all dignity keeping his children submissive, for if someone does not know how to manage his own household, how will he care for God's church? He must [13] not be a recent convert, or he may become puffed up with conceit and fall into the condemnation of the devil. Moreover, he must be [14] well thought of by outsiders, so that he may not fall into disgrace, into a snare of the devil.* — 1 Timothy 3:1-7

I have organized these fourteen qualifications into six categories, as follows:

- Public Character
- Marital Purity
- Positive Attributes
- Negative Attributes
- People Management
- Faith Maturity

Category One | Public Character

This category examines the first and last qualifications, focusing on public character:
- Above reproach.
- Well thought of by outsiders, avoiding disgrace and the devil's snare.

Spiritual leaders are not perfect. They are always growing, so these qualifications aim not for perfection, but for progress. Effective leaders assess and address their flaws, confront difficult issues courageously, maintain consistent character, and navigate various contexts with integrity. Their sound reputation stems not from a focus on reputation itself but from their character in both public and private life.

Category Two | Marital Purity

This category addresses a single qualification:
- The husband of one wife.

This phrase, when understood in the original language, means being a "one-woman man." It emphasizes moral and sexual faithfulness, applicable to both married and unmarried men. This understanding includes moral faithfulness in a marital relationship and sexual purity for unmarried men. Paul's intent is to have leaders who are morally and sexually pure, whether married or single.

Category Three | Positive Attributes

Here are five essential positive attributes:
- Sober-minded.
- Self-controlled.
- Respectable.
- Hospitable.
- Able to teach.

Spiritual leaders must act rightly, guided by God's Word. They are aware of their deficiencies and actively address them, take their ambassador role for Christ seriously, and use their talents to teach others about Jesus. These attributes reflect a man deeply obedient to Christ.

Category Four | Negative Attributes

Leaders must avoid these four negative traits:
- Not a drunkard.
- Not violent.
- Not quarrelsome.
- Not a lover of money.

A disciplined leader controls his desires, emotions, and actions. He steers clear of worldly vices and maintains composure in challenging situations, setting boundaries and exercising discipline.

Category Five | People Management

This category includes a single, vital qualification:
- Manages his own household well, ensuring dignity and submissiveness in his children.

Effective leadership at home often reflects one's ability to lead elsewhere. It requires investment, influence, mentorship, and understanding the unique personalities under one's care.

Category Six | Faith Maturity

The final qualification is:
- Not a recent convert, to avoid conceit and falling into the devil's condemnation.

Spiritual maturity does not necessarily correlate with the length of one's faith journey. Leaders face tests against pride, learning to recognize and resist its manifestations.

Evaluate which category or qualification you need to focus on. Addressing this could enhance your qualification as a spiritual leader. The church needs more leaders, and growing qualified leaders starts with individuals willing to step up. Pray, seek counsel, and engage actively in your spiritual growth.

MINISTRY: FUNDAMENTALS FOR THE SPIRITUAL LEADER

Leadership, particularly spiritual leadership, presents a unique set of challenges that often seem overwhelming. It requires navigating through complex situations with wisdom and a deep connection to God's will. This journey is vividly illustrated in the experiences of Timothy under Paul's mentorship, as outlined in 1 Timothy 4:11-16. Paul's advice to Timothy is invaluable, serving as a timeless guide for spiritual leaders confronting various trials.

Fundamental One: Character

"Let no one despise you for your youth, but set the believers an example in speech, in conduct, in love, in faith, in purity." — Timothy 4:12

Paul places immense emphasis on character, especially for young leaders like Timothy. The realm of leadership is fraught with challenges, but maintaining godly character is pivotal. Character is the bedrock of effective leadership; it's about how you speak, act, love, demonstrate faith, and uphold purity. In a world where leaders are often judged by their strategic prowess or tactical achievements, Paul redirects our focus to the core virtues of integrity and godliness. These traits are what truly define a leader's worth and impact.

Your character speaks volumes more than your age or your experience. Even in the face of mistakes or setbacks, a leader with a steadfast character remains unshaken. This principle is crucial in spiritual leadership, where the stakes involve not just human perceptions but spiritual truths and eternal impacts. Consider the leaders who have left a positive legacy; it's their character that outshines their strategies or methods.

Fundamental Two: Scripture Engagement

> *"Until I come, devote yourself to the public reading of scripture, to exhortation, to teaching."* — *1 Timothy 4:13*

Paul's directive to Timothy to prioritize scripture cannot be overstated. In the current era, it's easy for spiritual leaders to get lured away by contemporary ideologies or management systems. These might seem appealing and effective, but they pale in comparison to the transformative power of God's Word. The Bible is not an ordinary book; it's a spiritual tome that offers profound insights and divine guidance. Its role in leadership is not just informational but transformational.

Engaging deeply with scripture is foundational for every spiritual leader. This engagement involves more than just reading; it encompasses understanding, meditating, and applying God's Word in every aspect of leadership. As Paul emphasizes in 2 Timothy 3:16-17, scripture is 'God-breathed' and is essential for teaching, reproof, correction, and training in righteousness. By anchoring leadership in Scripture, leaders align themselves with God's wisdom and direction.

Fundamental Three: Embrace Your Gift

> *"Do not neglect the gift you have, which was given you by prophecy when the council of elders laid their hands on you. Practice these things, immerse yourself in them, so that all may see your progress."*
> *— 1 Timothy 4:14-15*

Paul's reminder to Timothy about his spiritual gift is a call to recognize and utilize the unique gifts bestowed by God. Many leaders confine themselves within the boundaries of their own abilities or resources, often overlooking the extraordinary potential of divine gifts. These gifts, when embraced and nurtured, can lead to remarkable outcomes that surpass human limitations.

This principle challenges leaders to step out of their comfort zones and trust in their God-given abilities. It's about leaning into the spiritual gifts and allowing them to flourish, guided by faith and trust in God's plan. The outcomes of relying on these gifts are often beyond what can be achieved through mere human effort or intellect.

In embracing and utilizing these gifts, leaders not only achieve greater feats but also exemplify the power of faith and reliance on God. This approach resonates deeply with those they lead, inspiring confidence and trust in divine guidance.

As we reflect on these fundamentals, it becomes clear that spiritual leadership is a journey that transcends conventional wisdom. It's a calling that demands a steadfast focus on character, a deep and unwavering connection with scripture, and an embrace of the unique gifts God has given each leader.

Leaders facing overwhelming situations can find solace and strength in these principles. Focusing on these fundamentals doesn't just provide a survival strategy; it paves the way to thrive in leadership. This approach impacts others profoundly while staying true to God's calling. It's about leading with a heart aligned with God's will, a mind enriched by His Word, and actions inspired by His gifts.

In conclusion, spiritual leadership is not merely about navigating through challenges; it's about transforming them into opportunities for growth, impact, and deeper faith. By adhering to these fundamentals, leaders can guide others effectively while fostering their personal spiritual journey, ultimately leading to a life that glorifies God and fulfills His purpose.

MINISTRY: 3 CHALLENGES TO EXPECT IN LEADING MEN

Many new men's leaders wrongly believe that spiritual leadership is easy. The opposite is true. Being a follower is so counter-cultural that we should expect just the opposite—more challenges and obstacles than we could ever imagine on a multi-dimensional level. Regardless of your age, wisdom, or experience, you will encounter them, and they will test your resilience.

But here's the upside: every challenge we encounter presents us with another opportunity for spiritual growth. Challenges move us from comfort to discomfort. They move us from control to trust. They move us from independence to dependence, all driving us back to God. And that's what God wants from us: total spiritual dependence on him, which results in spiritual growth. This is what you will see play out in 1 Timothy.

We will discover today that two men, Paul and Timothy, stepped into challenges together. Paul had been through many challenges, and Timothy was about to learn how. You will listen as Paul actively mentors and motivates Timothy to rise to his. I hope that you will see your challenges and rise to them in the same way. You are about to hear from one of the most resilient men in Christian history, and he is going to instruct, coach, correct, and encourage you all the way to the end of this series.

Let's look at the three challenges that Paul knows Timothy is going to face. They are all found in the first few verses of 1 Timothy 1.

One | Situational Challenges

> *"As I urged you when I was going to Macedonia, remain at Ephesus so that you may charge certain persons not to teach any different doctrine."*
> *— 1 Timothy 1:3*

Just like Timothy in 1 Timothy 1:3, you might find yourself in complex leadership situations that seem beyond your experience or comfort zone. You may feel underqualified or overwhelmed, much like Timothy felt in Ephesus, tasked with leading a church amid doctrinal turmoil and influential members. The key lesson here is the power of stepping up, despite feeling inadequate. It's in these moments that your reliance on God becomes pivotal. Your willingness to face these situations, trusting in God's strength and guidance, not only builds resilience but also demonstrates true leadership.

Two | Discernment Challenges

> *"As I urged you when I was going to Macedonia, remain at Ephesus so that you may charge certain persons not to teach any different doctrine,*

> *nor to devote themselves to myths and endless genealogies, which promote speculations rather than the stewardship from God that is by faith."*
> — *1 Timothy 1:3-4*

Timothy's challenge of discernment in leading the Ephesian church mirrors the discernment you must exercise in your leadership. You will face decisions that require distinguishing between truth and falsehood, making choices that align with your faith while navigating the complexities of guiding others. This journey of discernment isn't straightforward and often involves learning from mistakes and growing through experiences. Remember, as a leader, you're not alone in this journey. The Word of God, the Holy Spirit, and the fellowship of other believers provide support and guidance, enhancing your ability to make wise and godly decisions.

Three | Motivational Challenges

> *"The aim of our charge is love that issues from a pure heart and a good conscience and a sincere faith. Certain persons, by swerving from these, have wandered away into vain discussion, desiring to be teachers of the law, without understanding either what they are saying or the things about which they make confident assertions."* — *1 Timothy 1:5-7*

The final hurdle is the challenge of maintaining pure motivation. In leadership, it's easy to get sidetracked by personal ambition or recognition. Timothy was reminded by Paul to lead with motivations rooted in love and sincerity, steering clear of selfish desires. As a leader, your motivations should consistently align with God's purpose. It's a call to introspection and honesty, ensuring that your actions and leadership stem from a desire to serve God and others, not personal gain.

In your role as a men's leader, embracing these challenges is not just about personal growth; it's about setting an example of godly leadership. By facing situational difficulties with courage, exercising discernment in complex decisions, and maintaining pure motivations, you embody the principles Paul imparted to Timothy. These challenges shape you into a leader who not only guides others but also walks alongside them in the journey of faith and growth.

MINISTRY: DEALING WITH CONFLICT

In the realm of men's ministry, navigating conflict is an inescapable aspect. This might manifest as disagreements over strategic direction, mediating between staff members, handling disputes with peers, or even addressing issues with customers or suppliers. It's a multifaceted challenge that every leader faces. Those who shy away from conflict often find their leadership journey hindered, while those who embrace and adeptly manage conflict stand out as effective leaders. Here are some principles to consider the next time you're faced with conflict.

One | Manage Your Own Anxiety

It's crucial to recognize that conflict isn't inherently negative. In fact, it can be a catalyst for clarity and resolution of underlying tensions. The key is to focus on the issue without getting swamped by emotions. Conflict is essentially an issue in need of resolution, but with heightened emotions. By not getting emotionally entangled, you maintain the capacity to contribute positively to the resolution.

Two | Engage in Active Listening and Clarification

Heightened emotions can often derail effective communication. As a leader, your role is to cut through this emotional noise. This is done by actively listening and seeking to understand the core of what is being communicated. This approach not only provides you with a clearer understanding of the situation but also helps to calm the emotional turmoil of the parties involved.

Three | Identify Common Goals and Desired Outcomes

Often, individuals embroiled in conflict share common objectives but differ in their approaches to achieving them. As a mediator, identifying these shared goals can be transformative. It shifts the focus from the conflict to a collaborative pursuit of a shared outcome. This often involves backing up to see the bigger picture and finding a path that both parties can agree on.

Four | Establish Clear Next Steps and Accountability

Once a pathway forward is identified, it's important to outline specific, actionable steps. This might involve scheduling follow-up meetings, altering processes or protocols, or experimenting with new methods to circumvent the issue at hand. Ensuring clarity in responsibilities and timelines is crucial, along with setting up mechanisms for accountability to uphold commitments and decisions.

Five | Know When to Seek Additional Help

There are times when the conflict may be beyond your scope of resolution, either due to the nature of the issue or because it involves higher authority levels. In such cases, it's wise to enlist help from those with the necessary authority or expertise. This isn't a sign of weakness but of wisdom and understanding of one's limitations.

As leaders, we must understand that emotions, while a natural part of conflict, can obstruct clear thinking and problem-solving. Lowering the emotional temperature can pave the way for pragmatic solutions. Personally, I view conflict as an opportunity to guide individuals beyond their immediate emotional responses towards practical, mutually beneficial outcomes. It's in these moments that we not only resolve issues but also foster growth and understanding, both in ourselves and in those we lead.

MINISTRY: 4 POINTERS FOR PLANNING A MEN'S RETREAT

If you're reading this, you're likely a leader of men. I admire men like you, who actively engage in spiritual growth and aim to make a lasting impact. In our busy world, it's increasingly challenging for men to focus on spiritual development. However, a well-executed men's retreat can be a powerful catalyst for change in the lives of men, their marriages, families, and workplaces. As someone who plans such retreats, your role is vital. In my experience attending, leading, and speaking at men's retreats, I want to share some insights to help you avoid common pitfalls.

Here are four essential pointers:

First | Make a Commitment

Every successful retreat starts with a personal commitment from you, not your pastor, church, or a group of men, but you alone. It only takes one committed man to start a movement. Look at Jesus' example in the Bible; he was committed and gathered others around him. Your commitment to Jesus and the retreat is crucial. If you're not genuinely committed, men will notice and hesitate to join. So, ensure you're fully committed before proceeding.

Second | Assemble a Team

Once committed (and since you're still reading, I assume you are), you need a team. Gather a small group of about 3-5 men who are ready to embrace the retreat's vision and mission. At this stage, don't focus on assigning specific roles or tasks; these will emerge naturally. The key is to recruit men who are willing and able to invite others. The most crucial and often overlooked aspect of planning a retreat is recruiting participants. So, prioritize assembling a team capable of gathering more men.

Third | Determine a Structure

Begin by setting a time frame and work backward. Typically, retreats last 1-1/2 to 2 days, starting on a Friday night and ending on Saturday night or Sunday morning. Start by scheduling meals and meetings, the core components of the retreat. For a two-day event, this might include 5 meals and 4 meetings. Then, fill the remaining time with activities like competitions, games, and group discussions. Avoid over-scheduling; the aim is for men to feel refreshed, not exhausted.

Fourth | Determine the Speaker & Theme

Early on, identify a speaker who is both biblically knowledgeable and effective in communicating with men. Finding someone who excels in both areas is challenging but crucial for the success of your retreat. Avoid the mistake of assuming that a professional athlete or business leader with faith and a book automatically qualifies as a good speaker for your retreat. Once you've found the right person, collaborate with them to set the retreat's theme. Tailoring a program to a specific topic usually demands more effort and can be costlier, so it's practical to develop the theme around the speaker's strengths.

In conclusion, planning a successful men's retreat involves your personal commitment, assembling a dedicated team, creating a balanced structure, and finding a speaker who resonates with men. Follow these pointers to make a significant impact on the lives of other men.

GROUPS: 4 FAIL-PROOF WAYS TO KEEP MEN ENGAGED

Leading men's groups often comes with its challenges. I've experienced times when men didn't show up. But there was one year, believe it or not, when no one missed a single meeting. So, what was the secret to this success? It wasn't about using worldly tactics; instead, it involved returning to the early church's practices. Here are the strategies I used.

One | Use the Bible as Your Foundation

The early church didn't need to coax members into meetings. They were devoted to the apostles' teachings, as we see in Acts 2:42-47. When issues arose, such as the distribution of food, they resolved them without distracting from the Word (Acts 6:1-4). This commitment to Scripture not only pleased the group but led to growth and transformation.

So, how do we apply this? Ensure your men's groups are rooted in the Word. Whether it's a Bible study or a recovery group, the focus should be on scripture for genuine life change. This can be achieved through various methods – inductive studies, media-based resources, or, occasionally, reading a book together. But remember, the central focus should always remain on God's Word.

Two | Emphasize Mentoring and Discipleship

Align your studies with Jesus' Great Commission-to make disciples. It's not just about information, but transformation (Romans 12:2). As group members learn, they should become less worldly and more Christlike. This transformative experience significantly boosts commitment to the group.

Three | Foster Community Within the Group

The early church excelled in fostering fellowship. They ate together and met frequently, either in the temple courts or in homes (Acts 2:46). This kind of community, which includes sharing meals and meeting regularly, helps to build strong, meaningful relationships. It's about face-to-face connections, not just digital interactions.

Moreover, they cared for each other's needs, as seen in Acts 2:44-45 and Acts 6:1-7. This practice of supporting and looking out for one another strengthens the group's bond.

Four | Live with a Mission

Before Pentecost, Jesus outlined the church's mission in Acts 1:8. This mission was not just about evangelism but also about living out faith in the community. Small groups, while they might not have an ambitious global mission, are still part of this bigger purpose. A group focused beyond itself creates a compelling reason for commitment.

Five | Commit to Prayer

The early church was devoted to prayer, as seen in Acts 1:14. This practice led to powerful responses from God, like the coming of the

Holy Spirit (Acts 2) and miraculous events throughout the book of Acts. Prayer, especially focused on God's mission and glory, brings the group closer to experiencing God's presence, increasing commitment.

> *"Increasing dedication in our groups isn't about guilt-tripping members into attending meetings. It's about creating an environment that members value enough to prioritize. By embracing the foundational priorities of the early church, we can foster groups that promote life transformation, community, interdependence, and commitment."*
> *— Andrew Wheeler, author of "Together in Prayer"*

The key to fostering a deeply committed and engaged men's group lies not in compelling attendance through obligation but in cultivating an environment that naturally draws men in. By grounding our groups in biblical teachings, emphasizing transformative discipleship, nurturing genuine community, living out a shared mission, and upholding each other through prayer, we create a space that men not only want to be a part of but prioritize in their lives. This approach echoes the practices of the early church, proving that timeless principles can indeed forge strong, dedicated groups today. In doing so, we don't just gather men together; we build a fellowship that's deeply rooted in faith, brotherhood, and purpose.

GROUPS: TOP REASONS MEN DON'T JOIN MEN'S GROUPS

Few things positively impact us more than healthy relationships with other Christian men. And yet, still, so few men are engaged in a small group community. As a pastor who used to oversee small groups in one of the ten largest churches in America, Eagle Brook Church, in the Twin Cities, I can attest to the fact that involving men in small groups is the greatest challenge men's leaders, directors, or pastors will ever face. And we know that engaging men is a critical target market that often goes untapped.

David Murrow, the author of Why Men Hate Going To Church, said in an interview with CBN,

> *The pastorate is a men's club. But almost every other area of church life is dominated by women. Whenever large numbers of Christians gather, men are never in the majority. Not at revivals. Not at crusades. Not at conferences. Not at retreats. Not at concerts.*

While I think David's book title is a little extreme, the reality he paints in this statement is spot on.

More needs to be said about the root causes, mostly because we get disillusioned about the involvement of our men without understanding the real reason behind diminishing male involvement. Here are five reasons I believe men do not join small groups.

One | Man Struggle With Personal Shame

The first reason men don't join is that men deal with a lot of private and personal shame. While most men are not eager to talk about it, one of the primary reasons men do not connect with men's ministry or men's small groups is that they are embarrassed to admit that they may not have the answers. Men are sensitive about being made a fool of in a group meeting, whether they admit it or not. They also do not want to be the outcasts in a group setting. In moments of confession, I have heard men say personal shame or immature faith is a valid reason for avoiding small group engagement. While some people might want to shout, "Man up and get in a group," working through this issue is a real challenge. This is because men prefer to play on teams where they can win, do work they excel at, and be a part of group experiences where they can feel some measure of competence. So, do not ignore the power of shame by providing them with a safe and caring environment.

Two | Men Don't Respect The Leader

A second reason men don't join is that men don't respect the leader. While this is a tall order for any leader, this is a common reason for the lack of participation and followership. Men willingly and recklessly follow men who are perceived as strong leaders. They want to learn from them and want to sit at their feet. If someone like John Piper, Matt Chandler, and or the late Tim Keller walked up to you and said you join my group, you would probably follow. Because the character, wisdom, and leadership of the man make all the difference. There is no church with an army of incredible leaders leading the way, but there is usually one man who everyone follows. He is the one I would challenge to lead and replicate the men's efforts in my church, assuming his character is one that is biblically grounded and willing to lead.

Three | Men Don't Like Other Men In The Group

The third reason men don't join is that men don't like the other men in the group. Now, this is a typical chemistry problem. I have heard this excuse several times and have even had people leave groups I have led because there is some other man in the group that they do not like. I have also asked men to leave a group for the benefit of the group itself. This poses a unique challenge for any leader. We must remember that we will not always anticipate these issues; in some cases, we cannot avoid them. However, my solution has been to create groups with a broader reach. Here is what I mean: I have found that some of my best groups have been men who do not know each other very well. While most churches focus exclusively on having their congregation in a small "church" group, I've found that this is not always the best option for men. Groups with higher anonymity often have higher male participation at first because they can share more openly, and there is less risk with issues like chemistry. Just think about it: rather than having men exclusively from your church, how about having men from the many churches? Consider how this might increase the vulnerability and lower the risk for men who are not familiar with small group dynamics to begin with.

Four | It Doesn't Address Their Needs & Challenges.

A fourth reason that men don't join is that the group does not meet their current life stage challenges. A single man is going to self-opt out of a group for married men, and a group on fathering is going to exclude men who are not. While life-stage groups are helpful, they also create an issue for churches and ministries that are trying to get going. Often life-stage groups are challenging to establish unless you have a large ministry with a lot of good curriculum access. If you don't, then I believe focusing on common discipleship paths is much more effective. I have had hundreds of men join our program and use our small group curriculum for this reason alone: it attracts men of all ages and all walks of life with an extensive discipleship path.

Five | Men Are "Too Busy."

The fifth reason is the killer and a cop-out. As a leader who wants to see men mature, it drives me crazy when men proclaim they are "too busy." All our lives are busy. But I know one thing: life will never move as slowly as it does today. Therefore, I believe the excuse "too busy" is another way to say one of two things: either they did not want to mention one of the reasons above, or they prefer the status quo because life is fine as it is. What they are saying is that don't need it or want it right now. But I have discovered when the pain is high enough; they will reorder their priorities and consider that community, relationships with other like-minded men, and a regular dose of God's Word are just what they need.

Five Solutions For Your Men

So, in conclusion, while the obstacles are numerous, the solutions are out there because we cannot just give up. (And by the way, I have already given you a few great solutions to consider.)

For Shame – Offer a Safe Environment: Addressing personal shame requires creating a space where men feel safe to be vulnerable without fear of judgment. This could be facilitated through confidentiality agreements, an emphasis on listening without fixing, and encouraging openness by sharing personal stories of struggle and redemption by the group leaders. It's crucial to foster a culture where vulnerability is seen as a strength, not a weakness.

For Leadership – Strong Male Role Models: To inspire respect and engagement, choose leaders who embody the values and character traits admired in Christian manhood. These leaders should not only be strong in their faith but also relatable and approachable. They should be willing to share their own challenges and growth in faith, setting an example that encourages others to follow.

For Chemistry – Focus on Broader Community Engagement: To mitigate interpersonal conflicts, forming groups with men from diverse backgrounds and churches can be beneficial. This not only reduces the likelihood of pre-existing biases but also enriches the group with varied perspectives. Encourage a spirit of acceptance and understanding, focusing on common goals rather than personal differences.

For Life-Stage – Embrace General Discipleship: While life-stage groups have their place, a more inclusive approach is to focus on general discipleship that speaks to men at all stages of life. This could include topics like faith in the workplace, balancing family and career, and developing spiritual disciplines. Such groups provide a broad appeal and encourage mentorship opportunities between different generations.

For Busyness – Emphasize the Value of Community: Address the "too busy" excuse by highlighting the importance and long-term benefits of being part of a Christian community. Offer flexible meeting times, short-term commitments, or even virtual options to accommodate busy schedules. Make it clear that the group is a place of support and growth, especially during challenging times.

The journey to engage men in ministry is not without its challenges, but it is a worthy endeavor. By addressing the core issues that deter men from joining these groups, we can create environments where men feel safe, respected, and valued. It's about understanding and meeting their needs, whether it's through providing strong leadership, fostering a sense of community, or accommodating their busy lives. Ultimately, the goal is to guide men towards deeper relationships with God and each other, cultivating spaces where they can grow in their faith and as individuals. As we navigate these obstacles with wisdom and compassion, we pave the way for more men to experience the transformative power of Jesus.

GROUPS: THE INDUCTIVE O.I.A. METHOD FOR BIBLE STUDY

Let's face it. Many of us find the idea of personal Bible study daunting, especially if we haven't done it before. You might wonder, do you have to be a trained theologian to study scripture effectively? Absolutely not! While there are truths about God we may never fully grasp due to His immense greatness, His word is accessible and understandable to all of us, especially when we commit to studying it regularly. So, what's the secret to studying the Bible on our own?

Three Simple Steps to Bible Study:

One | Observation – What does the passage say?

This initial step might appear straightforward, but it's not always so simple. Often, we bring our own theological biases to our reading of Scripture, influenced by preconceived notions about what our theological framework should be. Remember, all our "grids" have their limitations. It's crucial to let the text speak for itself. Ask, "What does it say?"

Two | Interpretation – What does the passage mean? /Text

Here, the goal is to understand the author's primary thought or idea. Pay attention to the five C's: the context of the passage, cross-references where the Bible addresses the same topic (since using scripture is the best way to interpret scripture), the cultural context of the time, your conclusion about what the passage means, and, if needed, consult a commentary for additional insights. While this may sound complex, it's quite straightforward, and often the meaning becomes clear quite quickly.

← WHAT does it mean to ME

Three | Application – How does the passage apply to my life?

This is the stage where first-time readers often start, but it should be the culmination of the study. It's easy to appreciate the truths in Scripture, but applying them, especially the inconvenient ones, can be challenging. Yet, without personal application, Scripture study becomes futile and fails to honor God. The good news is that God blesses our efforts to align our lives with His Word. The Holy Spirit aids us in making this a reality as long as we are dedicated to taking God at His word and obeying His commands and teachings.

There's nothing more thrilling than discovering God, understanding His plan for our lives, and seeing His character shape ours. The book of Proverbs likens this process to a miner searching for silver and gold, reaping rewards after diligent effort. Every nugget of truth we uncover in Scripture is a treasure, rewarding us as we apply and live it out.

As you delve into your study of God's word, keep a journal to record your discoveries. Pray over these insights, asking God to help you apply the truths you've uncovered in your life.

What does it say
What does it say to other
What does it mean to me

GROUPS: THE S.O.A.P. METHOD FOR BIBLE STUDY

When leading other men in a Bible Study using the S.O.A.P. method, it's crucial to not only understand the process yourself but also to guide others in discovering its power and practicality. This method is an excellent tool for fostering deeper engagement with God's Word in a group setting.

Scripture: Guiding Others to Hear God's Voice

As a leader, encourage each man to engage with the Scripture actively. Choose a passage that is relevant and rich for discussion. When reading, invite the men to listen for a verse that resonates with them personally. Encourage them to write this verse down, reflecting on why it stands out. This practice helps each individual to recognize how God speaks uniquely to them through His Word. Remember, the goal is for each man to encounter God directly through Scripture.

Observation: Facilitating Insightful Discussion

In this step, guide the group to understand the context and message of the Scripture. Ask open-ended questions about the passage to stimulate thoughtful discussion. Encourage men to share their insights and listen to the Holy Spirit's guidance. It's important to create an atmosphere where men feel comfortable sharing their observations and understanding of the text. This step is not just about academic knowledge but about collectively seeking God's message in the Scripture.

Application: Encouraging Personal Reflection and Group Accountability

Application is where the study becomes personally relevant. Encourage each man to consider how the Scripture applies to his life. Discuss as a group how these verses can guide decisions, relationships, and spiritual growth. This step is crucial for personal transformation and accountability within the group. As a leader, share your own applications to model vulnerability and openness. Remember, the aim is to move from understanding to living out God's Word.

Prayer: Leading by Example in Conversation with God

Prayer is a powerful way to respond to God's Word together. Lead the group in a prayer that reflects on the passage of scripture studied. Encourage men to share their prayers, whether they be of thanksgiving, confession, or petition, based on the passage. Also, it provides a space for silent reflection, allowing men to listen to what God might be saying to them individually. Remember, prayer is an intimate part of the relationship with God, and as a leader, you're guiding men to deepen that relationship.

Expanding on the S.O.A.P. Method for Group Study

When using the S.O.A.P. method in a group setting, it's important to foster an environment of respect, openness, and confidentiality. Each man's journey with the scripture is personal, yet sharing it within the group can lead to collective growth and deeper bonds.

Encourage regular journaling as part of the process. This practice allows men to track their spiritual growth and reflect on God's work in their lives over time. As a leader, periodically revisit previous discussions to see how the application of God's Word has impacted the group.

In conclusion, leading men in a Bible Study using the S.O.A.P. method is about more than guiding them through a process; it's about nurturing a collective journey toward spiritual maturity. Through scripture reading, observation, application, and prayer, you're not only helping men to engage with the Bible but also fostering a community where they can grow, be accountable, and deepen their relationship with God. Remember, your role as a leader is pivotal in creating a space where men feel encouraged and supported in their spiritual walk.

GROUPS: A SAMPLE OF A 60-MINUTE S.O.A.P. STUDY

1. Welcome and Purpose (5 minutes)

The facilitator starts with a brief introduction, highlighting the group's purpose and discussing the guidelines for healthy, respectful discussions.

2. Regular Ritual (5 minutes)

Implement a short, meaningful ritual to transition from the daily routine to the focused setting of the Bible study. This could be a moment of silence, a brief prayer, or a simple group activity that sets the tone.

3. Introductions (10 minutes)

Each member introduces themselves and shares briefly why they are part of the circle today. This fosters a sense of community and personal investment in the group's activities.

4. S.O.A.P. Bible Study (30 minutes)

- Scripture (5 minutes): Read the selected Bible passage together and take turns reading it out loud so that men can hear it and process it.

- Observation (10 minutes): Facilitate a group discussion on the context, meaning, and insights from the Scripture.
- Application (10 minutes): Each member reflects on how the Scripture applies to their personal life and shares with the group.
- Prayer (5 minutes): Conclude with a group prayer, possibly including individual prayers related to the study.

5. Actionables (5 minutes)

Members share what they are taking away from the meeting and express gratitude for the insights and fellowship experienced.

6. Social Time (5 minutes)

Allow time for the men to socialize, discuss further any topics that resonated with them, or provide support to each other based on the discussions.

This structure ensures that the Bible study is central to the meeting while also providing ample opportunity for personal sharing, reflection, and community building. The S.O.A.P. method serves as the core around which the other elements revolve, creating a balanced and meaningful experience for all participants.

GROUPS: A STEP-BY-STEP GUIDE TO A FIRST GROUP MEETING

As you stand on the threshold of beginning your journey in a men's group, embrace this moment with intention and hope. Your first meeting isn't just a formality; it's the foundation upon which you will build your entire ministry to men. It's a sacred moment for setting the tone of what will hopefully flourish into a robust community and brotherhood in Christ.

The Prep (5 minutes)

Prepare the room so that when a man steps into the room, you'll be greeted by an environment that states "I was waiting for you." Things like coffee and donuts or beverages and snacks set a mood. They create an environment of warmth and hospitality. But it also communicates you have a plan and are leading a confined time frame. Most men don't think this is necessary, but it is. All the small things set the spiritual atmosphere for this time together.

Start with Prayer and Purpose (10 minutes)

Begin on time, and open with a brief prayer. Invite God to lead your time together and bless your fellowship. In the first few minutes, revisit your mission for initiating this group. It's crucial that every man understands the "why" behind the meeting. Share your heart, but more importantly, listen to how their "why" connects with yours.

Sharing Spiritual Journeys (30 minutes)

The next 30 minutes will be the heart of the first meeting. Give each man three-to-five minutes to share a snapshot of his spiritual journey. Encourage honesty and vulnerability. Whether someone is a seasoned believer or just starting out, reassure them that they are welcome just as they are. Warning: there are some guys you will have to cut off and other guys you will have to encourage to talk a little more.

Cast Vision and Encouraging Commitment (5-10 minutes)

With 10 minutes left, share the vision you have for the group. This vision isn't just yours; it's a shared canvas for all. Encourage the men that you're here to grow together, challenge one another, and support each other in your walks with Christ. Remind them that spiritual growth and fellowship don't happen overnight and that it's okay to 'test the waters' before diving in. This is where you will introduce the study or process you will use for the coming weeks.

Close With Prayer of Anticipation (2-5 minutes)

In your final moments together, pray for the men (by name) and the anticipation of the future of this group. Build spiritual enthusiasm for the time so men see this as their spiritual team meeting each week.

As you conclude your first meeting, remember that this is just the beginning. The seeds you plant today will grow into something greater than you can imagine. Your group isn't just about meetings; it's about building a brotherhood in Christ, a community where men can be real, grow in their faith, and support each other in the challenges of life. Embark on this journey with anticipation, knowing that God has incredible things in store as you walk this path together.

GROUPS: 10 CREATIVE FORMATS FOR A MEN'S SMALL GROUP

As a leader in men's ministry, you're embarking on a remarkable journey, one where your guidance can have a profound impact on the lives of men seeking to deepen their faith. The beauty of this journey lies in the freedom you possess to choose the format that best resonates with your group's needs and your unique leadership style. However, amidst this freedom, there are two crucial pillars that should underpin every group you lead: the enduring wisdom of the Bible and the nurturing of brotherhood among men.

The Bible is not just a book; it's the living, breathing word of God, a compass that guides us through every aspect of life. Your role as a leader includes helping men to dig into this rich source of wisdom, uncover its truths, and apply them to their everyday lives. Whether it's through in-depth study, reflective devotionals, or vibrant discussions, the Scriptures should always form the heart of your group's activities.

Equally important is the cultivation of brotherhood. In a world where men often feel the need to go it alone, your group should be a haven of mutual support, understanding, and encouragement. It's about creating a space where men can be vulnerable, share their struggles and victories, and forge deep, lasting connections grounded in Christ's love.

With these foundations in place, feel empowered to explore the variety of formats outlined below.

Here are ten creative formats for a small group gathering.

- **Testimony Trailblazers:** Here, each man charts his spiritual journey, marking the milestones of life before Christ, the life-changing encounter with Him, and the current walk in faith. It's a testament to the transformative power of Christ in every man's life.

- **Spiritual Summits & Slumps:** A group dedicated to sharing the ups and downs of their spiritual journey. It's a roundtable of resilience and revelation where men open up about their spiritual triumphs and tribulations.

- **Prayer Power:** This group embodies the power of collective prayer. It's a spiritual fortress where men gather to lift each other up in prayer, sharing their deepest requests and standing together in faith.

- **Devotional Diggers:** A group that delves deep into devotionals, unearthing the treasures of biblical wisdom and applying them to daily life. It's about mining the depths of God's Word for practical, actionable insights.

- **Leadership Lottery League:** In this dynamic group, every man gets a turn at leadership, bringing fresh perspectives and fostering a sense of shared responsibility. It's a leadership training ground rooted in scriptural wisdom.

- **Scripture Sojourners:** A journey through the Bible, one chapter at a time. This group focuses on unpacking the scriptures, encouraging a deeper, more personal connection with God's Word.
- **Breaking Bread Brotherhood:** Combining spiritual and physical nourishment, this group bonds over meals and informal spiritual discussions, fostering a unique camaraderie and fellowship.
- **Pulpit Pilots:** This group navigates through varied spiritual landscapes by hosting different speakers each week, broadening their understanding and application of biblical principles.
- **Visionary Video Vanguard**: Leveraging video sermons and teachings, this format offers a window to diverse theological insights and interpretations, enriching the group's spiritual journey.
- **Accountability Architects:** Focused on building a structure of personal spiritual growth and responsibility, this group tackles key accountability questions, supporting each member's commitment to living out biblical principles.

These creatively titled groups not only capture the unique focus of each format but also resonate with the journey of every man seeking to grow in faith and brotherhood, centered around the unifying power of scripture and prayer.

GROUPS: 6 EXPECTATIONS FOR EVERY MAN IN A SMALL GROUP

After three decades of small group leadership, I can testify that setting clear group expectations upfront creates clarity and healthier group experiences. While a moment like this will tend to feel authoritative for about ten minutes, this could be the most valuable 10 minutes for your group in the coming months. And here is why:

Ten minutes will save you tons of headaches.

The following six expectations have been a list I have built over many years of watching groups. Of course, you could build your own, or copy mine, but many of these I learned through the fire of common group issues I faced. Today they are a list that I read to all the men early on in a small group meeting. I do this long before I have an issue. This way, no man is singled out during or after some disruptive event.

I have found that reading this helps the men police themselves, and it welcomes them to contribute toward building a healthy group culture.

The Discussion Rule: Manage Your Conversation

- Everyone participates. No individual should dominate the conversation.
- When you are silent, you are agreeing, so speak up if you have something to add.
- Listen completely to understand the lesson and others' perspectives.
- Don't interrupt other men, but rather let them complete their thoughts.
- When you disagree, do so respectfully; consider using "I respectfully disagree."
- Speak to the topic at hand by guiding your mind and words.

The Personal Rule: Manage Yourself

- Expect challenge and tension, and it's okay if someone disagrees with you.
- Show up and turn off your devices.
- Communicate to the group when you are unable to attend.
- Be willing to be held accountable and admit when you are wrong.
- Grow in transparency and authenticity.

The Confidentiality Rule: Manage Confidentiality

- What is shared in the group stays in the group, but feel free to share your positive feelings about the group outside of the group.
- Your wife needs to know about you, not other members, so share your faults, not other's faults.

The Focus Rule: Manage Timeliness

- Respect the agenda by staying on topic and not trailing off topic.
- Stay engaged by writing down stray thoughts or questions that could take the group down a different direction than the focus for the time.
- Be present and ready to start and end on time.

The Spirituality Rule: Manage Your Discipline

- Read your Bible regularly.
- Pray daily.
- Take responsibility for your spiritual health and growth.

The Action Rule: Apply What You Learn

- Establish an action item for yourself each week.
- Take notes your way, and practice this as a pattern.
- Participate in the discussion.

GROUPS: BEST TO WORST SMALL GROUP LOCATIONS

This may seem unnecessary to address, but it's not. I believe the location of a small group discipleship experience with men can be a significant contributing or hindering factor. Recently, I met a group of men in a large church in a kid's classroom. While I was grateful the church let us meet there, this was a massive church with plenty of other adult places to meet. The chairs were made for kids, and I kept hitting my knees on the short tables. I think the leader ignored this detail, and while most were forgiving, it was a miss on first impressions.

The location of your small group impacts two things: first, the group dynamic, and second, your leadership. With conducive environments, these two elements are either delayed or accelerated, and I prefer removing the challenges from the start to make the whole process easier. I do this because constant distractions, access problems, or meeting issues will hijack a discipleship process and an entire week of time from you, and they can sometimes draw too much attention to your leadership faults and anxieties. While I think it is imperative to be transparent with your men, I have found that if I have less anxiety and can focus on leading the group when my anxiety lowers around one major factor: the meeting location. While my leadership flexibility is necessary, there are no constant meeting issues that distract from the relationships and content matter. And I have experienced it all in leading men's groups.

- The room is too hot or too cold.
- Another group is in our room.
- The door is locked to our room.
- The room is not set up.
- The power doesn't work.
- A group reserved the room half-way through our meeting.
- A person interrupts our meeting during a critical moment of sharing.
- The table breaks.
- The men cannot find the room.

Here is a quick list of general characteristics for you to consider as you pick a location. These are broad aspects, and then we will talk through examples of the best to worst locations.

First | Reservable

The first characteristic of a great meeting location is that it is a place that you can reserve. If you cannot book it or save it exclusively for your use, then you will probably run into issues eventually. I know this is basic, but having a long-term reservation is good. If you cannot reserve it, then you run the risk of being run out at some point, and this is not helpful for developing men as disciples. I remember one year we had to move our group four times, and while adventurous, this was not the preference.

Second | Right Location

I would make sure your location is in an area of demand for your men. In other words, ensure that it is within an area of reasonable driving distance. I have had men drive 45 minutes to one of my groups; however, this is not the preference. I would say about 15-20 minutes from each of the guys, and either their home or work is good. If there is much more distance, you will lose them, if not right away, eventually.

Third | Right Setting

The setting does make a difference. I have noticed this single factor contributes to accelerating or hindering groups more than any other. You are looking for an environment that is neutral and private. Therefore, I prefer a boardroom over a home and a private room over a public area. Fewer distractions to no distractions accelerate focus. Also, settings where you can sit in a circle at a round table, more than a rectangular table is best. Both work; remember, men will be able to see each other better at a round table. And yes, a table is necessary! I have led many groups without one, but men like to have a table to sit at for handbooks, Bibles, drinks, and a surface to take notes on.

Fourth | Right Sized

I have made the mistake of trying to cram too many men in a room. While this makes it feel full, when men cannot move around, it is distracting, hot, and uncomfortable when someone needs to leave early.

Fifth | Right Price

I have occasionally paid for space, but free is the key. Paying for space is not what you want to do, but sometimes you have no choice. And discipleship is worth it. Free is best, and there is always someone out there who will be generous.

So given these general characteristics, what are examples of the best to worst locations?

The Best Locations

The best sites are donated board rooms, training rooms, or community rooms with a door. All you must do is ask around. They often sit empty early in the morning or later in the evening. If you know a small business owner, I'll bet he has one. You can also contact your location church. I would say the critical requirements here are two. First, you want it free of charge. Second, you must have access without having to contact someone else. If the room is right and you can get these two requirements, then you are ready to go. FYI: I no longer use rooms or offices unless I have a key. When I cannot get into a room without someone else giving me access, it will, at some point, go wrong, and this creates anxiety for me. So I avoid it.

The Better Locations

The better locations are a restaurant with a private room and a low fee. Examples are coffee houses with separate rooms that charge a fee or require purchase. There are usually a number of these around town. They are very workable because men can get there early, buy their own beverages, and then join the group.

The Good Locations

Good locations are common areas with minimal distractions, like a library, school, or local government common areas. I have used all of these, and they are all free if you live in the area. However, coordinating them for a prolonged period can be a little tricky.

The Worst Locations

The worst locations are open areas like restaurants in the open. While I have been forced to use these, distractions are high, and without a private room, you cannot deal with individual and private issues. Therefore, men are less prone to open up.

In summary, remember you must choose at some point and live with what you have been given. But these are just the small lessons I have learned over the last few decades of small-group leadership with men. In the end, do it, and don't let the issues derail you as a leader. I would say learning to deal with the issues and problems of meeting space has made me a better leader and a smarter leader.

GROUPS: H.O.T. MEN MAKE STRONGER CONNECTIONS

We all know how easy it is for men only to have surface-level conversations that prevent us from experiencing the impact of genuine relationships. I think this can happen in any small group, even groups that are overly focused on Bible study. Let me share three essential principles that will take your small group to the next level and create authentic connections that will stand the test of time. I use the acrostic H.O.T.

Principle One | Honest

To establish a foundation of genuine relationships, we must embrace honesty. It's time to shed our masks and acknowledge that none of us have it all together. Because we need to be honest about our struggles, insecurities, and shortcomings, whether it's within our marriages, careers, spiritual journeys, or even with hidden sins. Growth begins when we are honest with ourselves and then get honest with God and our brothers. We discover a God who loves vulnerable men when we allow ourselves to be vulnerable. We also find freedom from our sins and encounter brothers who are eager to help us along the way.

One way to get men to be honest is to model honesty to the men in your group. By being honest about your own struggles and our victories, we inspire others to follow suit. So, invite men to be honest. Reward it when you see it. Lead by example so honesty can thrive.

Principle Two | Open

Being open is the next step toward creating authentic connections. What do I mean by being "open." Open men have lives that are like open books. They are unafraid of what others might hear or know about them. They understand that hiding is pointless and it's also dangerous, because it nurtures sin. These men are willing to be exposed because they know it's the best way to live.

One powerful way to foster openness is by allowing men to share their spiritual stories within the group. This exercise invites openness, allowing men to expose their hurts and hang-ups. Through this shared experience, we come to realize that we have all been lost, broken, and in need of a Savior. It breaks down walls and builds bridges of empathy and understanding that increase openness in others.

Principle Three | Transparent

Transparency takes us beyond openness. It invites us to share the secrets of our souls, even when we don't fully understand what's happening inside us. Transparent men take these courageous steps out of their comfort zones. They have what seems to be a reckless trust in God. They are willing to invite other men into a journey with them through their personal vulnerability. Men who are transparent are some of the strongest men I have ever met.

The power of transparency lies in its effects. It has an initial effect on a person but also creates a ripple effect in other people's lives. When one man shares the way transparently, others are attracted to this and inspired to do the same. The benefits of this include support, guidance, hope, and prayer, which far outweigh the concerns about gossip outside of a group. I have learned that it only takes one transparent man to crack the code of deeper spiritual connections and unleash the potential for transformation. When one man takes this step, usually others do too.

Our small group environments are meant to be transformative. I know the study is important. I want men, just like you do, to get into the content of the course and the Bible. But you must create an environment that takes the study beyond information. By embracing the principles of honesty, openness, and transparency (being H.O.T. men), we have the power to foster authentic connections that transcend those surface-level conversations. These principles will take men from information and behavior modification into transformation. So encourage men to aim for that H.O.T. mentality. And let's create environments that foster powerful connections and deep and practical transformation.

IN CLOSING: WHAT'S YOUR LANE?

As we draw the curtains on our journey, we stand at a crucial crossroads. It's a moment of decision—a time to step into the lane God has marked out for each of us. As I have often discovered in my years of ministry, knowing your lane and stepping into it with courage and conviction is the first step toward transformative leadership and discipleship.

Lane #1 | Be Mentored or Get in a Men's Group

For some of you, the next step is to immerse yourself in a community of like-minded men. Perhaps you've felt isolated or overwhelmed. Maybe you've been trying to navigate the complexities of life and faith on your own. It's time to change that. Joining a men's group or seeking a mentor is not a sign of weakness; it's a step of wisdom. It's about positioning yourself in a place where growth, accountability, and support are abundant. Don't wait for a crisis to seek help. Now is the time to engage, learn, and be ministered to.

Lane #2 | Mentor or Lead a Group

Others among you are ready to take the mantle of leadership. You've been equipped, either through life's experiences or through your walk with Christ. You don't need formal qualifications to lead; what you need is a heart for God and His Word and a willingness to guide others. Leading a group or mentoring someone isn't just about imparting knowledge; it's about being a living example of Christ's love and wisdom. Step into this role with humility and confidence, knowing that God equips those he calls.

Lane #3 | Develop Another Leader

The call to leadership isn't just about leading those who follow; it's also about raising up new leaders. Perhaps God is calling you to identify and nurture potential leaders within your group or your church. This is about investing in others, providing guidance, sharing experiences, and offering the support they need to grow into their own leadership roles. Developing another leader is a powerful way to multiply the impact of your ministry and extend the reach of God's kingdom.

Lane #4 | Develop A Leadership Team of Men

For some, the call is even greater—it's about building a team of leaders. This isn't about solo efforts; it's about collaborative, Christ-centered leadership. It's about gathering a group of men who can collectively shepherd, teach, and guide others. A leadership team brings diverse skills, perspectives, and gifts to the table, creating a robust and dynamic ministry environment. If this is your calling, pursue it with diligence and prayer, seeking God's guidance in selecting and nurturing a team that will serve His purpose in your church and community.

In each of these choices, the common thread is action. We are called not just to be hearers of the Word, but doers. The path of action you choose should align with where you are in your journey of faith and leadership. Remember, it's not just about making a choice; it's about stepping into the right lane for this season in your life.

As we part ways in this book, my prayer for you is that you will not only find your lane but will also accelerate in it with the power and guidance of the Holy Spirit. May your journey in men's ministry and leadership be fruitful, impactful, and glorifying to God. What will you do? The time to decide and act is now.

And I invite you to reach out to me or my team at any time. You are the men we are called to serve.

Your brother and fellow servant,

Vince Miller | *vince@beresolute.org* | **651-274-8796**